My Spirit-Filled Journey

From Rags to Riches

Relying on Jesus is always the answer!

Pray always!

Dawn Large

Dawn Large

ISBN 978-1-64349-313-8 (paperback)
ISBN 978-1-64349-607-8 (hardcover)
ISBN 978-1-64349-314-5 (digital)

Christian Faith Publishing, Inc.
832 Park Avenue
Meadville, PA 16335
www.christianfaithpublishing.com

Printed in the United States of America

Chapter One

We do not want you to be unaware, brothers, about those who have fallen asleep, so that you may not grieve like the rest, who have no hope. For if we believe that Jesus died and rose, so too will God, through Jesus, bring with him those who have fallen asleep. (Thessalonians 4:13–14)

I buried my mother today. I didn't know it would hurt this much. My heart feels like it's broken into a thousand pieces. I don't know if I could handle this. This is way too hard for me. I can't wrap my head around this. How can I deal with my mother's death when I can't even deal with death itself? Death always scared me. I didn't want to see my mother's body put into the ground. I asked for a sign from my mom. Please tell me heaven is real and you're there right now. The sorrow that flowed through me was unbearable. I felt like I couldn't breathe. I didn't think I would miss her as much as I did because we weren't close when I was growing up.

All the memories of how badly I treated her came flowing back. Like the times I didn't answer the phone whenever she called. She would call me, and instead of me picking up the phone like I should have, I let it ring, then she would call again and again. I would get angry when she called so many times, but I could have avoided all that just by picking up the phone. There were also many times I talked disrespectful to her. This didn't happen because of my youth; I carried these crimes into my adulthood. I felt sick to my stomach. The guilt I felt was horrible, all the, if-onlys. All the things I wished I would have done differently. This was the hardest day of my life.

I started to remember a day when I had fun with my mother. I was about seven or eight years old, and she was sitting on a chair in the living room. I was bored. I was lying across my mom's lap. I was in a giggly mood and talked about the silliest stuff, things that made no sense at all. I was laughing so hard I was crying. My mom started to laugh too. I was having fun making her laugh. I remember I used to ask her to scratch my back too, and she would. Then I remembered how close she and James became. When eating over watching her teeth go up and down almost coming out of her mouth. We would laugh at a lot of things she would say. These were the only fond memories I had as a child with my mother. These memories made me smile, and I found comfort in them.

The ceremony was beautiful. We had it at St. Mary's Church. It felt unreal, like she wasn't really gone, like I was going to get a call from her at any moment. My nephew Father Jack and a good friend of ours, Father King celebrated the Mass. Having them both there was very special to me. They were both there when Father King baptized my mom (she was born Jewish), and they were both there at the hospital when Father King gave her the anointing of the sick. Danielle was standing next to me in the pew. She seemed to be keeping herself together, but at one point she sat and cried. I hated to see her cry, but in a way, I was happy because then I knew she loved her. Seems silly that I thought maybe my children didn't love my mother. But I felt like that at times because of her mental illness. I knew James loved her. He was so good with her.

As Father Jack spoke about her on the altar, he had tears in his eyes, which made me cry more. Before Jack became a priest, he lived with us for a while. He used to play cards with my mom. They liked to play Rummy. My mom loved him, and I think Jack grew very fond of her too. Father Jack was very competitive and didn't let her win often. They had a lot of fun and laughs. Isn't it funny how others always saw her beauty and I remained a block of ice?

After Jack had moved out, my mother would ask about him very often. She would ask, "When is he coming to play cards with me?"

James also spoke about my mom. He read this at my mom's funeral:

> We are saying goodbye to a mom, mother-in-law, grandma, sister, but what I came to realize is that I am saying good-bye to a friend. We spent a lot of time together over the last few years, driving, singing, and talking.
>
> Elizabeth taught me so much about faith. Love and acceptance.
>
> She was a handful, but when I treated her with love, respect, and dignity that every human being deserves, I felt in line with God's will. When I was short, angry, and disrespectful, I felt very much that I was not doing God's will. I would repent, and she would unconditionally forgive, every single time.
>
> She suffered more mentally and probably even physically than any person I have ever met. Yet she was a woman of deep, almost childlike faith. In her struggles, she did not question God, but continually asked him for help, through her own simple prayers and the way she always asked others to pray for her. There were times when she appeared to be almost overtaken by her mental illness, yet she did not blame God for being sick but looked to him to be healed. "Pray for me that I could be well."
>
> Finally, I came to realize just yesterday one more thing she taught me. We would see her often, sometimes several times a week. When I would get to her room, the first thing she would say is "James, I miss you." I would reply, "Elizabeth, you just saw me three, four, five days ago, how can you possibly miss me?" She would always reply, "I love your company. I have to tell

you I didn't understand and would sometimes get a bit short." Well, Elizabeth, I just saw you five days ago, and I miss your company.

If you want to honor Elizabeth, tell those you love today that you love them, and say a prayer that she is before God, no mental illness, no physical ailments, and rejoicing for eternity.

I was so touched by his words. You could see him fighting back the tears. My mother was proud of having James as a son-in-law. She always spoke about him to the people in her adult home. Everybody knew everything about us. When we came to visit her, she would show us off to everyone. A year later, when I brought the headstone for my mom's grave, I put the usual things on it like beloved mother, Grandma, etc. But my husband asked me to put one more thing on it, "beloved friend." I thought that was so special that James thought of her not only as a mother-in-law but a friend too. I also put one of her sayings on the bottom of the headstone, "Momma loves you!" She said that pretty often.

Chapter Two

All good giving and every perfect gift is from above, coming down from the Father of lights, with whom there is no alteration or shadow caused by change. (James 1:17)

So many people came to say good-bye to her. She touched so many people's lives. She loved to make everybody laugh. My mom had a great laugh. She knew how to have a good time. I could picture her in her younger days being the life of the party. But I could also picture her hiding behind her laughter with sadness. I could see her goodness but her naivetés too. She trusted the wrong people because she was letdown by the one she should have trusted. She was so forgiving though. She truly loved her family and friends. She always had a smile on her face. She always looked happy.

She was the most loving, caring, and forgiving person I have ever known. I wish I would have realized that much sooner. For most of my life, I wasn't very nice to my mother. However, God gave me the most wonderful gift I could ever have. When she got sick, I was with her every day. I got a chance to take care of her and love her in a way that I never could before. God let me see her in a new way. I'm so grateful for that.

I saw how much my husband loved her too. He was so good to her. He loved her and took care of her better than I did. My husband even helped bath my mother, when she could no longer do it herself. Watching my husband with her was beautiful, and it made me love him even more. My mother's death was a big loss for my husband too. He too was at the hospital every day after work.

She never complained about her pain. She always said she was all right and always had a smile on her face. She loved everyone, even all the nurses and cleaning people at the hospital. She would speak Spanish to the cleaning ladies at the hospital. She knew a lot of Spanish because of the neighborhood we lived in, in New York City. She was afraid of doctors. She used to say they only want to use her body. But once she got to know her doctors, she loved them. She was just a bottle of joy. It would be great if you could bottle all the joy she had in her. I would open it often.

The day my mom died, I went to her assisted living home. I went to clean out the room that she had been in for the last seven years. I packed all her stuff up and placed it in my van. I felt sad saying good-bye to some of the people who worked there. She wasn't that far, the nursing home was the other side of the building, but I knew she wouldn't be going back to the assisted living part. After the van was packed, I went to visit her at her nursing home. I was carrying a bag with a few things I brought for her. She had lost a lot of weight and nothing fit her. So I got her a few new outfits, underwear, socks, and nightgowns. The last time she was in the nursing home before the hospital, they were doing physical therapy with her. She was afraid to fall. She had fallen a few times and hurt herself. She used a walker and walked very slow. At that time, I had thought she was going to get her therapy, start walking again, and go back to the other home. Little did I know that she was never going back.

It was a bright and sunny morning with a cool breeze. It was a nice day for February. It was only her second day back. I passed her room and just took a peek at her, she was sleeping. I went to see a woman to talk about getting my mom a hospice nurse. Besides my mom suffering with mental illness her whole life, she was diagnosed with terminal cancer. I told her she wasn't in much pain now and the doctor had told me she had maybe six months to live. I told her I wanted the nurse as soon as possible. I wanted my mom to be taken care of and make sure when the pain did start, the nurse would be there to give her pain medicine. They gave me some paperwork and told me if she had a hospice nurse she couldn't get physical therapy. I said, "Why can't she have both?" She informed me the purpose for hospice was to make a dying person comfortable, not to rehabilitate them. I didn't like the way that sounded. What if she got better? I just wasn't thinking right; it was wishful thinking that she would be fine for a few months before she got worse.

When I finished talking to the woman about the nurse, I went to see my mom. She kept going in and out of sleep. She talked to me a little bit. She was glad I was there. I told her James was coming to visit her tonight. That put a smile on her face. Then she nodded out again. I noticed her leg kept falling to the side of the bed. I picked it up and placed it on the bed and notice her leg was swollen. I mean, it was really big. I went to the desk and told them. They said I had to wait for the head nurse. They said they would get her. I went back to the room and the nurse was taking a long time, so I went back to the desk again. Finally, they got the nurse, and she came with me to see my mom's leg. The nurse looked at her leg and said this doesn't look good. She said she would call her doctor and keep checking it. She also said it was possible that she might have to go back to the hospital.

The first time she was in the hospital it was because she wasn't responding to anyone. And she was always walking around the home talking to everybody. When I got the call, they were taking her to the hospital, I met her there and James came too. We found out she had congestive heart failure, which swells up your legs too. She needed a blood transfusion. They said she had a heart attack also. After that she started to respond to us. While she was at the hospital, they were taking lots of tests on her. They found the cancer. I was in shock to find out. I didn't want to believe it. I thought with treatment she would beat this. The oncologist took more tests and told us the cancer started in the pancreas but it had spread to the liver and the doctor didn't recommend treating it. It might have given her a few more months to live, but they would be painful ones. Why would I put her through that. She had beaten breast cancer a few years back. They caught it right away, and they removed all the cancer. When she went back to the doctor, they said they had taken it all out and she didn't need to have treatment after. We were very happy about that. She had also fell in the home and hurt her arm bad, and she had huge black and blues. This was why she was afraid to walk after that and needed a walker.

So when the nurse saw her leg swollen, she thought she might be having heart failure again. We waited to hear from her doctor. I don't even think I talked to him. Things just started to go so fast by then. It seems like all a blur now. I was thinking, here we go again, back to the hospital, which I've kind of gotten used to. I thought they will fix her and everything will be all right for a while.

Then an aide came in to feed her. She needed to eat very mushy food because she lost her teeth in the hospital. She was starting to lose her appetite, which wasn't a good sign. She loved to eat and even enjoyed the hospital food. The aide started to feed her, but she didn't want to eat. Both I and the aide were trying to persuade her to eat. I told my mom she needed to eat to keep up her strength. The aide put some of the food in her mouth, but she wouldn't swallow it. She started groaning, and we told her to swallow the food. She wouldn't do it. I kept asking her to swallow it, but then she started to choke. I was getting nervous. My mom was struggling to breathe. I started to yell at her to spit it out. The food wasn't going down or coming out of her mouth. I kept on pleading with her, "Please just spit the food out!" The aide called in for help. They got a machine that would suck the food out of her.

All of a sudden there were six people in the room. One of them said to call an ambulance. My mom called out, "Danny, where is Danny?" still while choking on her food. It sounded like she was gargling mouthwash. "I'm right here, Mom. I am with you," I told her. I held her hand. They asked me to step back so they could get her ready to go to the hospital. I could see the color leave her face, and I knew something was wrong. My heart started to race. My body felt like it was heating up. The head nurse came in and listened to her heart and pulse. (Up until then, I really thought she was going to be all right. They would get her to the hospital and she would be fine again.) He ordered everybody to stop what they were doing and call off the ambulance. He told them she was a DNR. My heart dropped. Now I felt like I couldn't breathe. What does that mean? She can't get treatment! I didn't understand.

Having pancreatic cancer can be very painful, and it was too far gone to be treated. I couldn't bear to see her suffer, which is why I had agreed to a DNR, but I never thought that she would go that fast. Her doctor had told me she had maybe six months to live and possibly longer. I started to cry because I knew she was leaving me. I wasn't prepared to lose her right then and there. The last thing that she said was "Help me, God!" I could see the color of her face changing to a light gray. I knew she was going. My whole body was shaking uncontrollably. The nurse checked her pulse again and said, "I'm so sorry, she is gone." Then another nurse came to hug me; I began crying and collapsed in her arms. She just kept telling me, "I'm so sorry." They placed a blanket over my mother but not over her face. I couldn't move for a few minutes. I think I was in shock. This felt wrong; this couldn't be happening. This is not the way it was supposed to happen. No, we needed more time! She needs to wake up! James was not here. She couldn't leave yet without saying good-bye to James. I didn't know what to do. Then I went over to her and sat with her for a long time. I started to kiss her on the forehead, and I told her how sorry I was. I'm so sorry I wasn't a better daughter. This was all my fault!

I thought back at her choking on her food. I couldn't get the image out of my head. At one point, I wanted to tell the aide to stop trying to force my mom to eat. But I kept my mouth shut, thinking she knew what she was doing. I was asking my mom to eat also at first so she could keep up her strength. But she kept saying no and keeping her mouth shut. The aide just put food in her mouth while she was talking. It got me a little mad, but I still said nothing. For a moment, I had thought it was my fault she died because I didn't stop the aide from feeding her. I had to quickly get that out of my head. That would have haunted me the rest of my life, thinking it was my fault. I had to believe she would have died that day no matter what we did, and I didn't want to blame the aide for doing her job. She was only trying to help her. It was just my mother's time to meet her heavenly father.

At times I thought I heard her breathe, but the nurse said that was normal. I was still hoping she would get up. I was in shock. I couldn't believe my mom was gone. I don't know how long I was sitting there; it seemed like a long time. I just kept staring at her. She looked like she was sleeping.

God revealed a lot to me that day. Even though she wasn't the mother I thought I always wanted, she was the best mother I could have ever had. She loved me with all her heart and never judged me. All she wanted to do was spend time with her family. She was the best role model I could have. I wish I could be more like her. God showed me, even though I wasn't there for her most of her life, I was there for the most important times. She was able to see us more often when she moved to Jersey. We saw her for all the holidays, lots of weekends. When she lived in Brooklyn, we never saw her. But I was in a bad place then when it came to my mother. I was there by her side every day when she was ill. I was thankful to be there to say good-bye to her. She knew I was there in the room with her when she died.

I know her soul went right up to Jesus. My mom loved Jesus and would often ask him for help. I'm so glad she converted to Catholicism. And even though I didn't want her to leave me, I was thankful to God for taking her so quickly. She didn't have to experience the long, hard, and very painful suffering that cancer brings. We didn't have to watch the suffering. We were spared of that. My mom was finally in peace. She would no longer hear voices in her head. She will have no more pain. My mom was now with her mother, brother, sister, her two grandchildren, and Jesus in heaven.

I called my husband many times, but he wouldn't pick up his phone. It felt like hours passed by. I felt very alone. Numbness took over me. Finally James picked up the phone, and I told him that Mom was gone. He was in shock and started to cry. We both felt like this was all just a bad dream. He met me at the nursing home. He reached down and said to my mom, "You were supposed to wait for me." Then he kissed her on the head. I will never forget the words he said to her. I get choked up every time I think about it. We hugged each other and cried.

My mom lived in an assisted living (the other part of the same nursing home she was in), and all the people over there came to say their good-byes. They all told me great stories about her. How she helped take care of other people there. She brought joy to everyone who had the pleasure of knowing her. Residents, aides, nurses, and the janitor told me what a beautiful person she was. The janitor even had tears in his eyes. They all said they were going to miss her. It touched my heart to hear all the great things that were said about her. It was like I didn't know her at all until now. It felt strange but good to finally meet my mother for the first time. She was a whole new person to me. Now I got her, a little too late, but I got her.

She had a great sense of humor. She would have my husband and me hysterically laughing. She had certain phrases she used frequently. Like "Mama loves you!" "Generally speaking," "Pray that I should be well," "I enjoy your company," "That's unusual," "No funny business," and my favorite one, she used to say, "My daughter was no hanky-panky when she would go out with her boyfriend."

We had to call the funeral home, and we waited for them to pick her up. When the funeral home came, they asked us if we could say our good-byes so they could prep her to leave. I didn't want to leave her. How could this be? I thought she would live a longer life, like my grandma had. James held on to me as we were leaving. The walk through the hallway seemed longer than usual. I felt if I left that building, it was all over. The next time I would see her would be in a casket.

A lot of people showed up for her wake and funeral. It was heartwarming. I made a video of pictures of my mom to play at the funeral home. I cry every time I watch it. I got my mom a beautiful dress. She looked great in the coffin. I even took a picture of her. I wasn't going to show anyone that picture. It was just for me. God showed me what a great mother I had, and I'm very grateful for that. I didn't know that till then. I had a strange upbringing and didn't always like my mom. I'm glad God showed me who my mother really was. She had a beautiful soul. I'm thankful to God for giving me time with my mom and for opening up my eyes to her beautiful soul. When we went to the cemetery, there was snow on the ground, and we had to do the prayers inside. I didn't get to see her put in the ground, which kind of bothered me. It was a last and final good-bye. But at the same time, I didn't want the funeral to end. I didn't want an end to my mom. I prayed I would never forget her.

Weeks later, when everybody got back to their own lives, I expected everyone's life to stop. Don't you remember my mom died! Life can't go on! I know that sounds ridiculous, but that's the way I felt. Everybody needed to grieve like me. Life had to stop for everyone.

I started to miss all the annoying phone calls my mom made. The ones I never picked up. I used to save some of my family's messages. I looked for my mom's so I could hear her voice. There wasn't any! I don't know what happened to them. Maybe I had too many messages and they got erased. I was so upset! I wanted to be able to listen to her voice. She always left the same message. "Hello, it's me! Call me back!

I did get a call from her dentist, and they left a message saying she was approved for her new teeth. I saved that because it was a connection to her. If she would have lived, she would have had new teeth, which we would have been so excited about. Her teeth would always get loose and chatter when she ate. All of us were looking forward for that not happening again. Yet now I missed even that. For a long time, I would visit her grave once a week. It isn't that far from where I live. I don't go as much anymore, but when I pass by, I say, "Hi, Mom."

Chapter Three

You formed my inmost being; you knit me in my mother's womb. I praise you, so wonderfully you made me; wonderful are your works! My very self you knew. (Psalm 139:13–14)

My name is Danny Balin. But my family calls me Danny. I was born on April 26, 1965, to a twenty-year-old woman named Elizabeth Balin. She was a single parent. In fact, I didn't know my father at all. All I knew of my father was his name and that he had another family. I had half brothers and sisters I didn't know. I had another brother that I didn't know either, who was born two years before me. My mom gave him up because my grandfather wouldn't let her keep him. My grandmother tried to get him back, but the judge said she was too old (which was ridiculous, in my opinion, because she was only forty-four years old, I guess that was considered old back then). That must have killed my mom to have to give him up. She did get to see him a few times in the orphanage with my grandmother. Then they made her stop. We assumed he got adopted.

Even though my mother was very smart, after the eleventh grade, my mother dropped out of school. She hung out with the wrong crowd. Soon after, she got pregnant with me from another man. My brother and I had two different fathers. My grandfather couldn't tell her what to do anymore because she was twenty when she had me. She decided that she wasn't going to give up another baby. She decided to keep me and move out of her parents' apartment.

My mom told me that a man came to visit her in the hospital after she gave birth to me; she told the nurse she didn't want to see anybody. Whoever that was never came around again. It is possible that it could have been my father, but we will never know.

I didn't think about my father at all. I was never curious about my father or wondered what he was doing. I didn't feel the need to find him. I was used to being without a father. Even now I don't think about him. It would have been nice to have a father especially if he was a good man, then maybe I wouldn't have gotten myself into so such turmoil. But then I wouldn't have been the person I am today. And I learned good life lessons. It is what it is, and I don't dwell on that part. So I didn't have a father. No big deal.

Even though I didn't care to find my father, doesn't mean all children shouldn't have a father. A father is a very important part of a family. He is the head of the family. It is his job to take care and protect his family. So yes, I should have had one but I didn't.

Chapter Four

The Lord's face is against evildoers to wipe out their memory from the earth. When the just cry out, the Lord hears and rescues them from all distress. The Lord is close to the brokenhearted, saves those whose spirit is crushed. Many are the troubles of the just, but the Lord delivers from them all. (Psalm 34:17–20)

My mom was short (but everybody in my family was short) and very attractive, with long brown hair, blue eyes, and a beautiful smile. She probably didn't feel beautiful because of the way her father treated her; my grandfather didn't treat my mother good. I had heard stories of him holding her hand and him digging his nail into her cuticles. He would take his two youngest girls places. But never took my mother anywhere. When my mom needed anything for school, like a book, or if she needed a new pair of stockings because her old ones were ripped, he wouldn't give her any money for anything. But he was a big gambler and came home most of time with no money. The other kids didn't have it good either. But as they got older, they stood up for themselves. I think it was because they had stronger personalities. She also had two failed relationships.

My aunt Liza, at the age of twelve, would cook for the family. My grandfather was giving nobody money, and he was getting worse. My aunt Liza had to do a lot for the family. She would make the phone calls for bills. She had to be the strong one in the family because my grandmother was so timid. Liza became the mother of the family. She had to grow up fast and take on big responsibilities. Liza got a job at the age of fifteen still while going to school. She would buy the food in the house. She took care of her sisters and her mother. My aunt Liza was the one who threw my grandfather out of the house. He didn't listen to my grandmother when she would ask him to leave. My mom was nineteen when he finally left the house. My whole family had a hard life.

My mom found an apartment in Williamsburg, Brooklyn. It was a three-and-a-half-room apartment. She got it furnished through welfare. It was just the two of us for one and a half years. I was told she took really good care of me. She took me everywhere she went, and she would dress me up in the cutest little outfits. My aunts and grandma would visit; they loved playing with me and spoiling me. And sometimes my mom would take me to visit Grandma. We didn't live in the greatest of neighborhoods. My mom made sure I was loved and safe. My mom was friends with the landlord of the building we lived in. My aunt told me she was a very good mother. I was told my mother had a good singing voice, and she was well-liked.

My mom eventually became mentally ill. I remember being in a crib when two men came into our apartment and held her down. She was screaming. I'm not quite sure what happened, but this memory has haunted me for a long time. Our apartment also got robbed; they took everything, even pictures. A lot of things started to go wrong. My mom would take me out in the middle of the night, and she wouldn't let anyone touch me. My grandmother told me my mom put her hand through a window in our apartment. She was bleeding and needed stitches. My mom's concerned landlord called my grandmother and told her the things my mom had been doing and how out of control she was becoming.

Grandma then decided to take us into her apartment to live with her. My grandmother's apartment had five and a half rooms, with three bedrooms. My mom just got worse. My mother didn't talk for two years. She was catatonic; she didn't move. She was diagnosed with schizophrenia. My grandmother must have been beside herself with worry. What happened to her daughter? Her daughter that was once normal was having some sort of breakdown. She was totally a different person. The family must have been in shock. That was the beginning of my grandmother's suffering. She already had no husband anymore. It was a blessing she had children to help her get through this time. My mom was very young, and my grandmother was a nervous and timid person to begin with. This is not how a mother wants to see her daughter. I never thought about how this affected my grandmother until now. I understand how devastated she must have been. Now being a mother and having two handicap children of my own (which you will learn about later on in this book), I didn't understand what was going on at the time. I could only imagine I must have been scared.

Chapter Five

Look upon me, have pity on me, for I am alone and afflicted. (Psalm 25:16)

When my mother started talking again, she would ask, "Who is that cute little girl?" Her family would tell her, "That is your daughter." She would say, "I don't have a daughter." My mother denied that I was her daughter for about six years. I don't remember most of those years, I was too young. But I had to be a little confused. Think about it, I lived with a good mother for one and a half years. I had a mother who loved me and used to hold me and put me to sleep. At that time, I must have wanted her but got no response for two years. After that, I probably got used to it. My aunt Liza had to take care of me. At one point, my mom got violent and tried to stab my aunt's boyfriend. She never tried to hurt anyone else. She didn't like Liza's boyfriend. She used to say he is black. But before she got sick, she wasn't a racist. She loved all people. Eventually, she was put on a better medication, but she was still bad.

My mom would walk in circles and talk to herself, waving her hand around, trying to get the voices out of her head. She looked like she was being tormented. When she talked to herself, she would say that it was witches in her head telling her to do bad things. She would curse and become verbally abusive to the African-American people in our neighborhood. She would even spit on them. That was the end of any kind of normal life for me. No father and a mentally ill mother. Life didn't start out so good for me. But even so, I always had a roof over my head, food to eat, clothes on my back, and family who loved me.

The children in the neighborhood started to make fun of her, which hurt me very much. I also felt embarrassed and angry. I wished she wasn't my mother and would run away when she came outside. Some of the children would throw cans at her. I was only a child and didn't understand what was going on. I knew my mother was different, but I didn't understand what mental illness was. And why were kids so mean that they would throw things at her. The crib memory was fading as I got older. The only memories that I have of her are of her being ill. I don't remember my mom before she became ill. After her not talking for two years, now you couldn't shut her up. She just said all the wrong things. As I was getting older, it felt like I had a huge boulder just sitting on my chest. The heaviness of having a mentally ill mom was not an easy thing to live with. Every time she came outside and I was with friends, my heart would start to pound and my hands got sweaty and all I wanted to do was hide under a rock and never come out.

It was very hard for me and the whole family. Nobody could have a conversation with her. You would start to talk to her, and she would start out answering you back but then would talk to herself again. It was very frustrating, trying to bring her back every few seconds. It would go on and on till no one wanted to talk to her anymore. My grandmother would yell at her to stop, but she couldn't. And we could never bring her places because she always would be cursing her demons. My grandmother took my mother to all her doctor's appointments; she didn't have a car so she had to take the bus. My grandmother would get scared when my mother would talk about African-Americans on the bus. She thought someone would try to hurt her. I think she was a little embarrassed too. People would stare at her. Sometimes I would have to go with them, and I would feel the same way. At times I wouldn't sit near them so nobody would think I was with them. It was horrible walking through the city streets with her. I felt like I was being tortured. Looking back, I can see all the demons around my mother. I felt them without even knowing what they were. I know what evil feels like.

Chapter Six

I lived with my mom, grandmother, Uncle Dave, and two aunts, Liza and Sheila. My mom was put on new medicine, and she started to know who I was again but was still talking to herself. By then I was a little older. I never called her "mom" back then. She didn't feel like a mother to me. My grandmother and aunts took care of me all the time. My grandfather was already thrown out of the house mainly because he was a gambler and a womanizer. He used to sing at nightclubs. He even had a stage name. I didn't see my grandfather much. He would come around every so often and give me five dollars. I wasn't close to him because he was never around. He had a girlfriend which none of us liked. He wound up dying from diabetes. He was found in his apartment on the floor. His legs were blue and there were feces under him. Apparently, he was on the floor for a few days alive, but he couldn't get up. He obviously didn't take care of himself, and where was his new girlfriend? She was nowhere to be found. I was born on his birthday.

My uncle Dave was a great man! There was such a goodness in him. I was very young and don't remember a lot about him, but I had a feeling of purity and honesty. He was in the army, and he would come back with presents for me. He brought me back a beautiful Vietnamese doll; I loved it! My two aunts wanted to see it, and they both yanked it out of my hands. The doll broke, and I was so mad at them. They were more like sisters to me than aunts. I liked tunnels, so one day my uncle Dave rented a car so we could drive though the Holland tunnel. He was always tickling me. To this day, I hate being tickled, but he was the only one I have ever let tickle me. He always made me happy. I was very excited every time he came home.

I was crossing the street one day (I was too young to cross the street, but I saw all the other kids do it). I looked around the corner and didn't see any cars. We live on a one-way street, and it was curved. I started to cross when I got hit by a car. It must have been going fast because I didn't see it. The car hit me and my whole body went under the car. I was on my back and saw under the car as it rolled over me. The only thing that happened was the tire went over my toe. The driver came back to see if I was okay. They offered to take me to the hospital. I screamed and wouldn't get in the car. My uncle came down and he calmed me, so I went in the car with him and my grandma. I had a broken toe. They put my toe in a liquid bath, and I started to cry; it hurt so much. All they could do after that was just bandage it; you can't put a cast on a toe. I went home and laid on my or my grandma's bed. They gave me ice cream. That was my first miracle. I got hit by a car and lived to talk about it.

My aunt Liza was going out with this guy, who my uncle Dave didn't like. One day my aunt's boyfriend Hank was sitting on the couch with his pants undone. My uncle Dave came in and saw him and started to yell at him for sitting like that in front of me and the other women in the house. He said he was being very disrespectful. He told him to get out of the house. My mother wasn't the only one who didn't like Liza's boyfriend; Dave wasn't very fond of him. Dave being the only man in our family, he felt he needed to protect us. He and my mom were right about Hank; the rest of the family just didn't see it till much later.

One day I was playing with this tiny straw that you blow bubbles though. I was six years old at the time, there was a knock at the door, and my grandmother answered it. All I could hear was my grandmother crying. I didn't know what was going on. I found out my uncle Dave was dead. He had just finished his tour in the army, and it was his first day back to work. On the way to work, his car hit a pole, and he died instantly. I don't remember crying, although I felt very sad. I loved my uncle very much. I always felt so safe around him. He was my hero. We sat Shiva, a Jewish tradition honoring the dead, meaning we sat on boxes for a week, and we had to cover all the mirrors, which scared the hell out of me. I thought if I looked into the mirror, souls would come out. I was afraid to even go near the mirrors, let alone look at them. We had many guests that visited the family and gave us food. Later on, my grandma told me he didn't want to go to work that day. My grandmother told him to stay home but he went. See my grandma thought that was a sign that he shouldn't have gone.

No one explained death to me. Death was a very scary thing in my eyes. One night when I was in bed, I felt someone touching my feet. When I looked up, no one was there. I got scared and put the covers over my head. It happened again. I thought it was my uncle. Later my aunt Sheila had told me she was sleeping in her mother's bed and saw Dave. He was wearing a collared button-down shirt, like he wore to work. He was telling her to go in the other room but not to tell Mommy. She was too scared and just closed her eyes. For a long time I was afraid. I was afraid how it felt to stop breathing. I remember thinking, *Would it hurt to stop breathing?* Will I be scared at the time of death? And it also scared me that I wouldn't be able to think or dream. I will always remember my uncle Dave; he was very talented. I found drawings in his closet. I loved looking at them; they gave me comfort. I often wonder how my life would have been like if he was still around, probably a lot different. But things happen for a reason. Now I believe he is watching over me.

My aunt Liza became like a mother to me. She was the one who disciplined me. She was the one I was afraid of. All she needed to do was look at me in a certain way, and I would shut up. She spanked me when I was bad. It wasn't often because I was a good girl for the most part. But I did do some stupid things a few times and deserved what I got. One day, one of my friends wanted candy but did not have any money, so she decided to steal some at the grocery store. I took one of my aunt's pocketbooks, and we went to the store. She convinced me that I should be the one who actually stole it. I was so scared, but I did it and got caught. The manager went on the loudspeaker and asked if anybody knew me. I was so embarrassed. My neighbor was there. She took me home and told my aunt Liza. I got a spanking for that one, right in the hallway on the floor we lived on. I didn't even get to the door of the apartment yet when I saw her coming toward me. I vaguely remember my grandfather in the hallway as well. I guess he was visiting.

Another time, one of my classmates, whom I was afraid of, made me play hooky in first grade. I had a nickel, and she took it from me and told me if I cut school with her she would give me back my nickel. We went to the park and were playing in water when this girl told me I should take off my watch (which was given to me by my grandmother's boyfriend); when it was time to go home, the watch was gone. Boy was I in trouble! I got home to late, didn't go to school, and lost my watch. I don't think I even got my nickel back!

Aunt Liza also loved me very much. I was very shy, and when anybody came over, I would hide behind my aunt Liza. I was very attached to her. She would buy me things because my mom was on welfare and couldn't afford to buy me nice things. She would get me new school clothes and school supplies. She would take me shopping with her; sometimes we would walk for hours. All I wanted to do was go back home; my feet hurt. She was like the energizer bunny, always on the go. Loved to shop and get good deals. We would go to Central Park and the zoo. It was fun spending time with her. She introduced me to the theater. She would take me to off-Broadway plays. Some were so small, I felt like I was part of the play, but I loved it. We went to a ballet and magic shows. It was really a blessing that she introduced me to all of the arts. It was a life safer for me, and I think she knew that, having a mother who was mentally sick and couldn't do any of those things with me. She was a great cook too! She would cook Spanish rice and beans that were so good. I liked almost everything she made. I didn't like her liver, yuck! She tried to cook it different ways and not tell me it was liver, but I always tasted the liver. One day she had friends over the house. I think I was supposed to stay in my room, but I came out and saw them all smoking pot. I didn't know at the time it was pot. She dressed like a hippy back then, with a leather headband around her forehead, bellbottom pants, and a very colorful shirt. Later on, she learned how to make clothes with a sewing machine; she would just buy different patterns.

Chapter Seven

Be brave and steadfast, have no fear or dread of them, for it is the Lord, your God, who marches with you; he will never fail you or forsake you. (Deuteronomy 31:6)

We lived in New York City, and when I was seven years old, we moved to Brooklyn. My grandma wanted to get the family out of the bad neighborhood we lived in. Someone got stabbed in front of our building once. I think it also made my grandma sad to be in the New York apartment because she had memories of her son being there. My aunt got new furniture and new rugs for our new apartment. We had a red rug and plastic on our furniture. We had a nice dining room set. I used to play under the table, it was my cave. The floor was water and the furniture was rocks. I would jump from rock to rock trying not to fall into the water where sharks were and get in my cave where all my dolls were. Since I was an only child, I had to use my imagination a lot. The apartment was a nice size, three bedrooms, a kitchen, bathroom, dining room, and living room. Not long after we moved, Liza moved out to live with her boyfriend Hank.

My mother was a heavy duty smoker and would flick her ashes a lot out of nervousness. She burned holes in our rug and couch. And one day set her bed on fire. The fire was next to her head. We had to take out the burned plastic off the couch and get rid of the rugs. There were wood floors under the rugs. I would love running and then sliding across the floor. After two years, Liza moved, the apartment wasn't so nice anymore. She would come by from time to time and clean the house for us. She did what she could but needed to live her own life too. She took care of me as much as she could by taking me on the weekends.

My other aunt Sheila brought home two cats, and we already had one. I was allergic to them. I would get so sick, my eyes would get red and itchy and my nose all stuffed. I learned that I couldn't touch the cats and they couldn't go in my room. My aunt Liza got a cute puppy that looked like a little German shepherd; he was a mutt and didn't grow much. He was a small dog. She wound up leaving the dog at our house because the dog was chewing on her stuff and Hank got mad at the dog and kicked it. I would lie on the floor and he would lick my face and it tickled and I would laugh. I loved that dog; he was with us for a while, but one day when I got home from school, he was gone. My grandmother said she couldn't afford to keep him and the cats. I was really upset. I was allergic to the cats and couldn't touch them, but I wasn't allergic to the dog and she got rid of it. My aunt Liza really got rid of it; she said that was the plan when the dog came to stay with us. I didn't know that. His name was Koby. I never forgot that dog.

Grandma put me in summer camp. I cried because I didn't want to go; none of my friends were going to camp. But she wanted to keep me off the streets. I would hang out on my block. We lived in a two-family apartment and a door down from us was a big apartment building where most of my friends lived. When I started camp, it was weird at first because I didn't know anyone. But as I kept going and making friends, I started to love it. I was picked up every morning and dropped off at dinnertime. Three days in the summer, we would have a sleepover at a dude ranch or camping site. I had a crush on a boy named John Quinn, and I was very shy around him. At the ranch, we were getting ready to ride horses, when this boy said sometimes the horses bit you and there was a horse close to my leg while I was on another horse. I started to cry and told them I wanted to get off the horse. I never got on a horse again. And when we were camping, we would try to sneak off to the boy's side. I had a few great summers. My grandma paid for camp for three or four years. I was disappointed when she couldn't afford it anymore.

Not too long after my aunt left, my grandmother moved into her boyfriend's apartment; his name was John. I don't really know how she met him. I remember he was a bus driver for the New York transit. One of his stops was on the corner of my building when we lived in Manhattan. Grandma knew when he would be stopping there, and we used to meet him. I would jump on the bus, give him a kiss, and get off. I liked him. He would buy me nice things, and I thought he was rich. He was a big drinker and wasn't always nice to my grandmother. He was very nice when he wasn't drinking. She moved about an hour away. You needed to take two buses to get to her. When I got older, I would travel to see her and walk 86th Street with her. It was a very busy street in Bay Ridge, Brooklyn, with lots of stores. It was always crowded. There was double parking everywhere. John hung out in a bar right around the corner. Grandma would bring me to see him. And I remembered it was always during the day. He must have retired by then or it was his day off.

But now I was left alone with a mother who was mentally sick and Aunt Sheila whom I used to have fistfights with. Basically, I was on my own and did whatever I wanted. My aunt Liza got married to Hank, and they let me stay with them sometimes. They would take me to plays and camping trips. I loved staying with them. It felt like we were a real family. I wanted them to adopt me. My uncle Hank was so funny and nice, and I wanted him to be my father. I loved them both very much.

My aunt Sheila got pregnant. She had a beautiful baby girl named Charlene. She was so adorable! I used to babysit her, and so did my mother, which shows you the state of mind my aunt Sheila was in. One of the times I watched her, she fell down the stairs. I didn't realize the door was a little open. I was so scared I held her so tight and started to cry. I was afraid to look at her head, thinking her head cracked open or something bad like that. I never did tell her mother. She only got a small bump on her head, thank God.

Charlene was very smart; at a very young age, she was already reading. I loved Charlene very much, but my grandma would always tell people how smart she was. I started to hate hearing it. My grandmother made me feel very small and insignificant. I knew my grandmother loved me, but I always felt like I didn't measure up to her standards.

I have some good memories of Grandma. I loved the way she took care of me when I was sick. One of my best memories was her rubbing Vicks on my back and neck when I had a cold. Even after I got married, every time I got sick, I would call my grandma. It could be in the middle of the night, and she would talk to me and make me feel better. Another great memory is of her letting me sleep with her sometimes. She always had chocolates under her pillow. I used to love touching her face; it was so soft. She did worry about me a lot. But she worried about everybody in her family.

I wished that I was smarter. I wasn't a good student in school. I didn't read well and later on found out I had some learning disabilities. My aunt Sheila would try to help me with my homework. She would call me stupid all the time. So that was how I saw myself. I thought very little of myself and was ashamed of who I was. I had very low self-esteem. I was embarrassed to read in front of anyone; at school, I would never raise my hands. I wasn't a good reader and read very slow. I never played board games that you had to read. I was afraid of not knowing a word. When we had class spelling bees, I would raise my hand and tell the teacher I had to go to the bathroom, and I would stay there a while.

When I was younger, Sheila was always nice to me and fun to be around. She was my funny aunt, and I liked to be around her. She introduced me to my best friend Cathy. Somewhere down the line, something changed in her. She became very bitter. No one in my family got along with her anymore. She was mean. She hit my mother once and made her cry. I wasn't very close to my mom because of her illness, but when I saw my mother cry, it killed me. That day, I hated Sheila. We fought all the time. Sheila found a new man and married him. I think it was because he needed a green card. He turned out to be a jerk. Sheila put him before her own daughter and that wasn't okay. She was smart but could never keep a job for long. She was hard to get along with, so she would get fired. Later on she was living in shelters and on the streets.

I also had another aunt who passed away from asthma. Her name was Lacey; she had two kids, Abbey and Carl. I spent a lot of time with them when I was younger. We drifted apart when I started hanging out with my friends. Lacey was a very sweet aunt; she always called to see how I was doing. Aunt Lacey never left her house, and she was a hoarder. She would order everything she liked from QVC and kept everything still in boxes. She was found dead in her bed. Grandma and I went to the house and the cop was at the house. The ambulance came, and it took a while to get her out. She was surrounded by all the stuff she bought. My aunt Liza and I helped her husband clean out the house. We found loads of money in her closet. I can't help thinking that if she would have left the house and got exercise and fresh air, she would still be alive. I got socks and underwear from her every birthday and on the holidays and sometimes hats and gloves. I never ran out of that stuff. My aunt Lacey was very generous.

I got a small job in a pizza store. It made me feel important to have a job. I only worked there for a very short time. But it gave me some confidence in myself. It was also nice to make a little money. The owner was very nice in the beginning. Then he started to try and touch me in inappropriate places. He scared me. I never went back there, and I never told anyone, yet again another disappointment in my life. Was there ever going to be anything good in my life? Would I always feel this emptiness inside me? My family was dwindling down to nothing; everyone had left. I walked around aimlessly, wondering if life could get any harder. I was feeling ashamed of who I was and where I came from. Life itself scared me, and I thought I would never be able to ever be happy. I had no confidence in myself whatsoever.

There was one good thing in my life; I had my best friend who lived on my block, Cathy. We spent a lot of time together. She was thin with straight black hair. She was older than me, so we were in different grades. She was smart. I liked hanging out at her house because she had a mom, dad, and two sisters, a real family. I thought that was what a normal family looked like. She had to do her chores, go to the store for her mom, and go to church.

I had no responsibilities. I came and went whenever I pleased. Sometimes we would hang out at my house; we would be in my bedroom looking out the window at everyone who went into the bar next door. Sometimes we would throw pennies at them and then slip back in the window. Once we threw a penny and it fell in a man's beard. That bar burned to the ground three times. Since it was attached to my building, we would wake up with smoke in our house. The firemen would come, and we would have to wait in the street in our pajamas. I was told that they burned their own bar for the insurance money. Cathy and I had a lot of laughs together. I think she was my only friend I let come into my house.

Chapter Eight

Cathy and I used to walk two long city blocks to the junction all by ourselves. It was a safer time back then, or so we thought so. The junction was two avenues that came together. There were many stores there. We would walk there for McDonald's or Baskin and Robin's ice cream. There was a Burger King right across the street from McDonald's. You were able to get in or out of Burger King on either side, Nostrand Avenue or Flatbush Avenue, that was the corner that connected both avenues. And in McDonald's, you could also get to the other street, Camp Road. Campus Quarters was an arcade that we would go to. Brooklyn College was down that block along with Midwood High School. The train station was down the junction. It was the first and last stop at that station. Mornings were very busy in the junction, everybody trying to get to school and work on time. There were many bus lines too.

Across the other avenue was a Jewish bakery. My grandma would go there every Friday and get challah bread. The bread was yellow and soft inside with a shiny brown crust. The bread was delicious; it was sweet. I looked forward to Friday's for the bread and butter.

When we got older, we would buy clothes at the Joyce Leslie store. I loved that store. There was a jewelry store called Michael's, where I got my first ring from my boyfriend, James. It was a double heart ring with our initials on it with four little diamonds. We would also go to the college movie theatre; I think it only cost one dollar to see a movie there. And a few blocks down was a store called Stallions where we would get our drugs from.

One day, Cathy told me she had to move. I was very upset; she moved to Benson Hurst. I had to take a bus to visit her. I met a guy named Kenny there whom I really liked. He was Cathy's boyfriend best friend. He asked me out, and I said yes. I would go to her house every weekend to be with him. We would hang out at Cathy's house all the time. We went to see *Saturday Night Fever* at the movies. I loved that movie, and I loved John Travolta. We hung out where they filmed the opening of *Welcome Back Kotta*, which John Travolta was in. I really liked Kenny; he was so sweet. Cathy's older sister had a pot party one day (the day I first smoked pot). I was already smoking cigarettes at the age of eleven. I went out with Kenny for about a year but ended up breaking up with him.

I used to go to Mass with her and receive Jesus on my tongue. I was Jewish and didn't know that I wasn't supposed to do that. I liked going with her to church. One morning, I had a fight with my aunt Shelia. I got so upset I didn't want to go to school or stay home, so I walked from Nostrand Avenue and Avenue J to 85th Street and Bay Parkway. It took all day. I had no money on me, so I couldn't take the bus. When I finally got there, I told Cathy what happened. Her mother let me stay a while and then gave me money to get back home on the bus.

Another time, I had a fight with Shelia was when I was invited to Cathy's sister's wedding but I was late getting to her house. I didn't have anything to wear, so I wore a blouse and skirt that was my grandmother's. I wound up getting into a fight with Shelia, and she tore the blouse in the front. I was so upset on the bus to Cathy's house. I arrived at Cathy's house in tears. Her mother gave me a nice pin to hold the blouse together. It was right in the middle so it looked like a fancier blouse with the pin on it.

I spent a lot of time at Cathy's house. We would sunbathe in her front yard, putting baby oil all over us. We went to the beach one day with my aunt Liza, and we were lying on our back staring at cute boys. We stayed there too long, and the backs of our knees got so burnt and our backs as well. We were in pain the next day. Cathy lived there for a few years, and then she told me she was moving again, this time it was to Florida. It was going to take a little more than just a bus to get to her. My heart was broken! I loved her. We did everything together. I loved her family. I missed her and her family very much when she left.

Chapter Nine

Trust in the Lord with all your heart, on your own intelligence rely not; in all your ways be mindful of Him, and He will make straight your paths. (Proverbs 3:5–6)

I didn't always make the right choices, but even at my worst, I was searching for something. My heart was always good. When children around me would make fun of other children with handicaps, I would hate that. But I was also too afraid to stand up for them. I didn't like treating people mean and always respected older people. I didn't like confrontation. If an older person yelled at me, I would cry. I was a follower, not a leader. In high school, there were these men handing out little tiny bibles. I took one and started to read it. I liked it, until I got to a part I couldn't understand, so I stopped reading it. But I was very curious about Christianity. I wanted to know more, but my life got in the way of that. The kids I hung out with were my neighbors. We all had problems one way or another. I tried to ignore mine, like it wasn't there. Like when I would run away if I saw my mother in the street. Everybody knew she was my mother, but if I wasn't there, it never happened. Most of my friends came from broken homes. We dealt with things the best way we knew how to. Some liked to drink too much, some drugs, others were bullies.

I had another friend, Doreen, who lived in Benson Hurst. In fact, I hung out with three Doreens in Benson Hurst. I liked her brother, and I would flirt with him. We started to see each other secretly. The reason for that was that he was seventeen or eighteen, and I was only twelve. I really liked him; he was very cute. And it was exciting being with an older guy! It didn't last long though. One day I went to his house, he told me his mother wasn't home. We were making out on his bed, and he started to open up my pants and I kept saying no. He kept telling me how much he liked me and continued to try. At one point, I started to get scared. He was strong and was holding me down. I got myself in another jam! God must have been watching over me that day because his mother came home and caught us on his bed. She started yelling. She said to me, "Get out of here and go home." I went home and never saw him again. She called me and told me I should stay away from her son because he was too old for me.

I would cut school, and I would smoke pot every day. I was only twelve years old. I was asking people on the streets for money to buy nickel bags. One day I was smoking pot with my friends, and I started to strip. One of my friends stopped me; I fell asleep and didn't even remember doing that. I would steal money from my aunt Sheila. I stayed out all hours of the night. I was a big flirt! I loved getting attention from boys. No one paid attention to me at home, so I had to get it somewhere.

I would eat over all my friends' houses because we had no food in the house. I didn't want to be home anyway. I think my friends' mothers felt bad for me. I would never ever invite people to my house. My house was very dirty. My aunt Liza was the only one who would clean the house, but she was gone. I had holes in my kitchen walls. We had roaches, and no matter how much we sprayed to get rid of them, they were always there. Our landlord wasn't a very nice person and never fixed anything in our house. Maybe if we had a man in the house, things would have gotten done.

I started hanging out with the three Doreens; I used to go to the *Rocky Horror Picture Show* every Thursday with them. One of the girls asked me to stay with her at her cousin's house. I stayed there all summer, and nobody knew where I was. We did whatever we wanted to do. My aunt Liza finally found me. I locked myself in the bathroom. I was afraid to come out. I said, "If I come out, you're going to hit me!" Liza said she wouldn't, but I didn't believe her. I finally opened the door, and she smacked me. I knew it! That was the last straw; my aunt had to become my legal guardian and take me to live with her in New York City. I told her the only way I would move with her is if I could keep smoking, and she said I could. I was mad, I really didn't want to go, but I had to go. After a while, I liked living with her; it felt like we became a real family.

Chapter Ten

Say to those whose hearts are frightened; Be strong, fear not! Here is your God, He comes with vindication; with divine recompense He comes to save you. (Isaiah 35:4)

It was summer in New York when I went to live with my aunt Liza and uncle Hank. Years prior to this, when I was still living at home in Brooklyn, my aunt Liza and uncle Hank came to visit me and my grandma. While I was watching TV, lying on my couch, my uncle came to lie next to me. I didn't think anything of it. We talked for a while. Then my uncle grabbed my hand and put it on his genitals. I moved my hand away, and he took my hand again and started to rub my hand across his genitals. I started to get scared. I told him to stop, and he told me to just rub it. Finally, I got the courage to get up and run to the room where my grandma and aunts were. I wasn't going to tell them at first. I tried just to start talking to them like nothing happened. They looked at my face and could tell I was afraid. My aunt Liza asked me what was wrong. I said, "Nothing." She said, "I know you and something is wrong." I told them all what happened. My aunt's face got furious looking. But I knew telling them was the right thing to do. My aunt started screaming at Hank. Hank said nothing happened, and she took him home. I felt sick!

The very next day, Hank called me on the phone; he was crying. He said he was sorry and he would never do anything to hurt me. He also said he was drunk, and he would never drink again. I believed him and cried too. I still think he was sorry. He really did care and love me. So life went on, he stopped drinking, and everything was great again between us.

Now back to living with them in the summer. I was older now, and my aunt got me a summer job at the board of education. I would take a bus to work. We used to go to this public pool now and again, and I met a boy there. I thought he was very cute. I started going to the pool club more often because of him. One day at the lockers, I and this boy started to make out. My uncle Hank came in and saw it. He was so furious! He grabbed the boy and said to him, "Stay away from her. If I see you near her again, I'll kill you." I still saw him in secret for a while, and then it was over. A few weeks later, I met a boy that lived in my aunt's apartment building. We were together for a while, and then I found out he was moving. I was very sad, even started to cry. I really liked him. He was so cute, and he was also very nice. He never tried anything with me. We kissed hello and good-bye, but that was it. He was a complete gentleman.

Now that I was older, I was starting to develop. One night while I was sleeping in the living room, something woke me up. I opened my eyes; they were a little blurry from just waking up, and I saw my uncle Hank walking away in his underwear. I got scared, and I looked down at my pants. My pants were undone. I couldn't sleep the rest of the night. I tried to convince myself that it was just a dream, but it wasn't. My uncle had started drinking again. He was a very jealous man. If another man just looked at my aunt, he would flip out. He would hit my aunt at times. He had held her out of the window by her neck, and we lived on the twenty-first floor. He scared me. Hank would get home from work shortly after I got home. He started to feel my breasts every time I was home. He would tell me my breasts were bigger than Liza's. I was scared to tell my aunt this time. I didn't know what he would do. On another night, I was sleeping in my aunt's bed; he was working nights. He came home and wanted to have sex with my aunt. She told him repeatedly to stop, "Abby is in the bed." I was up but made believe I was sleeping. I was so scared, I wouldn't move a muscle. He made her have sex on the same bed I was sleeping on. On that day, sex became dirty and bad to me. One day, I just sat behind another building and started to cry. I looked up, not even knowing why, the sky was so clear that day. I must have been talking to God. I said out loud, "Why is he doing this to me! I love him. He is like a father to me!" I was afraid to be in the house with him alone, so after work, I would go to my aunt's friend's house to play with her little kids and talk to her. Then when I knew my aunt was home, I would go home. I couldn't believe this was happening to me. My world was falling apart. My heart was crushed!

Summer was almost over, and I still never said anything to my aunt about Hank. A few days later, we were all in the car going somewhere and we stopped and Hank got out of the car to get something at the store. My aunt asked me what was wrong. "You have been acting different these days. You're not laughing at Hank's jokes anymore." I told her nothing was wrong, but she didn't believe me. She asked again, and I told her. She told me to not say a word to him. She would take care of it. A few days later, she drove me back to Brooklyn to live with my other aunt that I hated and my mentally ill mother. That was the end of family life for me. I was heartbroken. What would life be like now? I had many friends in Brooklyn, but I felt so alone. My aunt wound up leaving her husband. She became clinically depressed. She had to be put in hospital for a short time. For a while, she couldn't talk to me on the phone. She was too ashamed of what happened to me with her husband. She finally called and talked to me, and we both cried. My aunt got better and moved to Brooklyn. She wound up finding a nice guy, moved in with him, then they were married. She had a baby boy named Donny. They lived in Queens, and I would visit them. I liked her new husband, James. Hank wound up dying from something, maybe cancer. Never did have any closure with him. I forgive him; he was a sick man with many addictions and couldn't control himself. I wish he would have gotten the help he so desperately needed. Before he died, he had remarried, and I think she wound up leaving him. So he never got the help he needed. Maybe right before he died, he made it right with God. I could only hope. But now my aunt was safe and happy, which made me happy.

Chapter Eleven

I went back to my old ways. Started hanging out with neighbors, smoking, and drinking. I would cut out of some classes. I met a girl in my class named Theresa. I found out she hung out with the popular kids. There was a boy (yes, another boy) named James Slater, whom I thought was so cute. He was not at all like my other boyfriends. I used to like Italian guys, with greased-back hair, chains around their necks, and liked disco. I loved disco. This guy was very different. He liked rock and roll, wore T-shirts with rock bands on it, tight Lee's or Levi's jeans, had long beautiful hair, and had a scar over his eyebrow. His eyes were hazel, and his hair was dirty blonde. He took good care of his hair; nobody was allowed to touch it. He looked tough, and I liked it. Oh, yeah, he also wore Converse sneakers. I fell in love with him before I even met him. I would watch him play football on the street and look at him like a lovesick puppy. He was so cute, he made my heart melt. I would think he could never like me. But if he didn't, I did have a second choice. I really wanted James though.

I started to hang with my new friend Theresa and her sister Dena. I would sleep at their house sometimes. One day, Theresa and I were going up the elevator to her apartment, and a man came in with us. We were just talking to each other when Theresa started to look at me funny. She pointed her eyes toward the man, and I looked. He was masturbating and fully exposed. The elevator door opened, and we ran to her apartment. We told her mother's boyfriend, and he ran down the stairs to get him. He was gone. It was time for me to go home, and I was too scared to get in the elevator. So Theresa and her mom's boyfriend went down with me. The elevator door had a round window in it. They started back up, and I saw the man coming in the building. I ran to the elevator and started to bang on the window; it was already going up. I ran as fast as I could up the stairs screaming. Her mom called the cops. They wound up finding him, and we had to go to a lineup to identify him. We also had to go to court. He was put away. I was never so scared in my life. I saw that man's face in my dreams. After that, I was always scared to get in an elevator with any man I didn't know. Sometimes I would make-believe I was waiting for someone so I didn't have to get in the elevator with any man. Then when it came back down empty, I would get in it and go visit my friends.

Theresa, Dena, and I would get into mischief; more than a few times we stole pants at the flea markets and at the mall. We would put Jordache jeans under our coats and walk away. We didn't have enough money to buy them. We took a lot of them and a coat for Theresa as well. I even stole some money from my aunt Shelia. I took Theresa and Dena to a small amusement park. I spent the money on them and took photo booth pictures. We were supposed to be in school. Instead we spent our time goofing off. We had a great time. We were probably wearing the stolen jeans. We would wear our jeans so tight we had to lie down on the bed and use a wire hanger to zip up our pants. It just didn't feel right wearing loose pants. We even wore our sweatpants tight. When my aunt would ask me where I got the new pants from, I told her they were Theresa's pants and that we borrowed each other's clothes. She believed me. Once we went to the mall with a few other girls and stole some stuff. Someone noticed, and we started to run. I never ran that fast in my life! One of the girls got caught, the rest of us got away. Even though I would steal stuff, I was always scared of being caught.

Getting back to James, I told Theresa I liked James and she told him. A few days later, he asked me out on the corner that we hung out on; we were sitting on a car. I said yes. I was a bit shy and didn't know what to talk about. I asked him if he ever saw the *Rocky Horror Picture Show*. I didn't know what else to talk about. We really never talked to each other before that. We hardly talked after that. We didn't know each other very well; we were really strangers to each other.

We would all hang out on 34th Street dead end, but the girls would be together talking in one crowd and all the boys were together in another crowd. We would only get together with our boyfriends at night to say good-bye; we would all pick a car to lean on and make out with our boyfriends. Weird relationships we had. I could talk to any other boy except for James. I thought he was too cool for me. I think I was a little enchanted by him. The longer we got to know each other, the more we talked, but it took a while. I was infatuated with him. I thought about him all the time, maybe too much.

One night we were arguing about something (I don't remember what it was), and I started to cry. I have never cried in front of him before. James didn't like seeing me cry, and he held me and said it would be all right. I remember feeling so safe in his arms. I wanted to stay like that forever. He invited me to his house that day for the first time. I met his parents. I was very shy, but his mother was so nice. She made me feel at home. Later on, I became very close to her. When James and I were fighting, I would still go to visit her. I loved talking to her. I didn't have another grown up that really listened to me when I spoke. I fell in love with his family.

We hung out in cubbyholes and empty garages. We drank, smoked, and used very bad language. We hung out on the block where one of our friends lived. The cops would sometimes come down the block and everyone would drop their beers and joints. It was a little funny because we all did it at the same time. Then we would go inside the gate of our friend Billy's house, and his mother would tell them, "They are on my property." She was one of those mothers who didn't care that her underage son was drinking. She even drank with us. I thought she was cool at the time.

We would sneak into a pool at night, going under the fence. The building was huge. It looked to me like there were twenty floors, but I don't really know. I just know it was a very tall building, and I thought only wealthy people lived there. Someone jumped off that roof once. We would head down the train tracks. It wasn't a train for people, not sure what it carried. One of my friends said, "If they catch you down here, they will shoot you with a BB gun." Every time we heard the train, we would run. Around the corner on 35th Street, the boys would play football, and in the winter, the girls would put on their boyfriend's coat. I loved to wear James's coat; it smelt like him. And we would watch them play. I would find myself staring at James at times. I loved when he smiled or laughed. We hung out with a pretty big group of friends. I couldn't wait till the next day to hang out again.

James and I broke up a few times. Once it was because the other girls broke up with their boyfriends, so they said I should too. I didn't want to break up with him, but I was a follower, not a leader and I did it anyway. In between break-ups, I went out with other guys. I liked the attention; I craved it. One of the guys was James's ex-girl-friend's brother. He was cute and very smart. He used to call me and sing to me. He also said words I didn't understand and wrote me poems. That was ultimately the reason for breaking up with him. He was much too smart for me, and the songs and poems turned me off. I guess I liked the "bad boys." There were other boys too, but I always went back to my James. I even went out with one of his friends. I really didn't want to because we were good friends and I loved hang-ing out with him; he was very funny and always made me laugh, but he wasn't really my type. All the girls told me to go out with him and said that he would treat me right. I felt pressured into it. It was the worst thing I could do because when I broke up with him, it ended our friendship. I missed having him as a friend. I looked for other guys' attention because I didn't get the attention I wanted from James. At that time, his friends and drinking was more important. I went with another guy named Charles; he had his driver's license. He would pick me up in his mom's car. We went out for a few weeks. I really liked him. He was sweet and cute. When I told him I was going back with James, he got upset. One night, he was drunk and told me he was falling in love with me. That really killed me. I hated hurting him. James and I were meant to be together.

There was another boy whom I used to see with my friend Sissy. We hung out in the Sizzlers parking lot when we met. Another day, we went to hang out with that group of guys. I was sitting in a car with him, talking, and all of a sudden, we just stared in each oth-er's eyes. I swear it was like a Hallmark movie. It felt like we stared in each other's eyes for a long time. We started to move in closer and closer until our lips met. It was so romantic. But that didn't last either. James and I got back together for a short while and then broke up again.

Theresa and Dena had a New Year's Eve party. The house was filled. James and I were broken up. I told one of his friends I wanted to get back together with him. He said he would talk to James for me, and later on that night, he told me that James was going to ask me out again. James wound up getting sick and throwing up. He fell asleep on Dena's bed. I sat next to him and rubbed his head. One of his friends took him home. The next day, I found out that James's original plan was to ask his ex-girlfriend out. I was crushed! It was good for me that he got sick because he asked me out instead a few days later. No matter how many guys I flirted with or went out with, I always found my way back to James. He made my heart skip a beat.

One day I was hanging out with a few kids from 28th Street and went down the tracks. The tracks were filthy, and I didn't really like being down there. It was the first time that I drank vodka. James was working, so I decided to hang with a different crowd. I was drinking and didn't feel like I was getting drunk, so I drank more. That was a very bad idea! All of a sudden, I stood up and then I felt very drunk. I started to walk down the tracks with some girl, and we were laughing and then fell on top of each other. The other girls got up and started to walk back to the guys, and I tried to get up but couldn't. I felt so sick. I thought I was going to throw up. Then I heard people over me, it was James's friends: Kyle, Tim, and Miles. I was face-down on the tracks. I didn't even like sitting on the tracks, let alone lying on them. James's friends Kyle and Miles tried to pick me up, and I said, "No, I'm going to throw up on you." Kyle stayed with me a while and then said he would get me over to the others. I still didn't want to move, but he insisted and said he didn't care if I threw up on him. The other friends I was with left me there. Thank God James's friends came. They brought me to the others and laid me down on the ground. They put a coat over me and started to drink with the others. When it was time to leave, they pushed me up the hill, and by then Kyle was drunk. It was kind of funny because I had two guys on each side of me and Kyle in the back, then Kyle rolled down the hill until you couldn't see him anymore. They had to bring me up the hill and then go back to find and get Kyle up the hill. They walked me home. I never did throw up, but I felt horrible. I only tried vodka one other time, and I got sick again. It was at a friend's party, and they put the vodka in a watermelon with lemonade; it was delicious. That was the end of my vodka days. From then on out, I just stuck to beer.

We were still drinking on the streets. I would go to the corner we hung out at every day and just wait for people to arrive. They were home with their families, eating dinner and doing chores. I had no rules, no dinnertime; I would eat cereal, tuna fish, eggs, mac and cheese, hot dogs, or sometimes when we had the money, hamburgers for dinner. My go-to dinner was Chef Boyardee or Campbell soups. All the stuff that was cheap. My aunt Sheila used to buy her own food and not let us eat it. She labeled all her stuff and would hide canned goods in her closet. I would steal some of her food at times. She always knew when something was missing, but I always denied taking it. I became a good liar. I didn't want to be home because I felt like there was nothing there for me. I couldn't stand the filth. I would wait for hours for my friends, even in the cold weather. Looking back, I probably should have cleaned my house myself, but I was just a child and just wanted to get away from that house. Being with my friends and James was an escape from my family.

I hung out with a bunch of different friends. Some of the guys weren't nice to me, but I kept going back for James. One of the guys would call me a greasy Puerto Rican and asked me if I had owned a bar of soap. I was half Puerto Rican on my father's side. I always stood up to him, but everyone else was afraid of him. He was a big bully. He made me cry at times but never in front of him. They also made fun of my sick mom. I would get so embarrassed when she would come down the block in my shorts (that was too small for her, she was on the heavy side, she had a big belly), asking everyone if they had cigarettes. When I saw her, I would run down the block to tell her to get out of there and go home. She would continue to come to the block I hung out on. And every time I saw her come down the block, I felt that same feeling of shame. My heart was crushed by the fact everyone else had a normal family with a mom and a dad. Every time I saw my mother, I wanted to crawl under a rock. I can't even explain the pain I felt. It was like I was dying inside.

We hung out in the corner store and brought looseys, which was one cigarette for five cents, and these steak sandwiches that came in a bag and they would heat it up for us. Those sandwiches couldn't have been healthy for us, but they were delicious. We also ate a lot of Slim Jims too. The guys would play stick ball down the block, and they were on a baseball league for a couple of years. I loved to watch James play.

James and I were together for one year. He bought me a double heart ring. He threw it at me, and the box landed on the floor. He wasn't so romantic back then, but I love him and I loved my ring. By now all the girls were having sex with their boyfriends. I was the last one to go "all the way." James was a gentleman and never forced anything on me. It was me who initiated it. I was curious and all the girls said it was great. The first time, we were on a car and were kissing. I touched his leg and told him I was ready. The first time hurt a little, but after that, I was hooked on it. We were at the beach at night; we were eating clams and drinking beer. He got mad at me that night because he found out I told my friends we were sleeping together. He told me that it was nobody's business what we did and that should have been private. I told him I was sorry, and he forgave me. The next day, he came to the block with a rash all over his back. He said it must have been the raw clams he ate.

We were older now, and instead of hanging in the streets, we hung out in bars, but we were still technically too young to be in a bar. The owner didn't care. The place was a dump, but we were there every weekend. James would play Donkey Kong at the bar until they changed it to Joker Poker, which he won money on a few times. We would watch MTV at the bar, which was a big thing back then. That was the first time we saw music videos and loved them. He also liked to play darts.

James liked to drink. He also liked to play darts, which he was very good at. He, his brother, and some friends formed a league and would play at other bars. They won lots of trophies. Every week on the same day, as dart night, all of his brothers would eat at their mom's house before the game. It was always hot dogs, beans, and mac and cheese night. All the boys were close to their mother. I loved that about their family. Their mom was very important to them.

I used to ask James to come over to my house in the middle of the night. I had a door in my room that led to the hallway, so he would never go through the dirty house. Some nights, he would rather go drinking with his friends. He would walk me home, we would make out, and I would beg him to come in. Sometimes he would go back to his friends, drink a little more, then later would come knocking on my door. One day, we had sex in his house, and his mother caught us in the act, which was so embarrassing. I stayed away from his house for a while. I felt horrible because I really like James's mother. I saw her after in the street, and I got scared. She came over to me and told me to be careful, "You're going to wind up pregnant, and you wouldn't be the first one in the family." She said everything with a kind voice and hugged me after. I might have cried a little. But I started going over James's house again.

Things with my aunt Sheila and I got bad. We were fighting all the time. She wasn't nice to me or my mother. So I went to live with my friend Sissy for the summer. Sissy was so funny. She would have me in stitches. I was still underage, but her mother let me stay. I told her I wasn't getting along with my aunt. She said I had to be home by nine. One day, I was late, and her mother was worried about me. When I got home, I gave her some story about James being in a car accident. She believed me.

I started hanging out with Sissy's friends sometimes. She had a good friend named Linda, whom I became good friends with too. She went out with a boy from my building.

James's younger brother hung out with Sissy's crowd. He would tell me I should break up with James because he didn't treat me right. I knew James loved me. We had some problems, but I wouldn't give up on him.

Sissy and I did some crazy things together. One day, Sissy had a fight with her stepfather, and she locked the door to her room. Suddenly we saw smoke coming from under the door. He put her jeans between the door and the floor and set them on fire. He was trying to smoke us out. We opened the door and ran as fast as we could out of the house. Sissy realized she didn't have her shoes on, so I gave her one of mine. We walked and walked until a man in a car stopped to talk to us. We talked to him. He wanted us to get in his car, but we didn't. We were stupid but not that stupid. He showed us a roll of money and asked us if we were hungry. We said yes, there was an open store a few blocks away. He drove while we walked. On the way, Sissy and I were trying to come up with a plan to get that money, but we chickened out. We went to that store, and he bought us bagels and junk food. He got back in his car, and we started to walk. He wanted to hang out with us. I told him I had to go home, but if my mother was sleeping, he can come up. We went back to my house, and he parked the car in front. I said to him I would come back down to get him. We got in my house, and I locked the downstairs door and then locked all the doors to my apartment. He started to yell at the window, but we ignored him. He finally gave up and left. That was a dangerous game we were playing. He now knew where I lived. Even in the streets, he could have grabbed one of us. We did lots of crazy things. We had our guardian angels with us that day and many other days that could have ended in a disaster. We were friends for a long time with Sissy, but after she had her kids, she became distant. I tried to reach out to her at times, but she didn't respond.

Chapter Twelve

I wound up getting pregnant at an early age, and we decided to have an abortion. My mother was sick and didn't know she was signing a consent form for me to have one. A friend came with me. We took a train into New York City and went to the clinic that performed the abortion. I was scared, but I was so young and didn't know anything about what I was really doing. Like many people today, I wasn't sure it was a baby yet. When I woke up after, I was dizzy and lightheaded. I remembered there were rows of beds with girls on them. It was a little unsettling. I felt like it was a chop shop. They gave me something to eat and sent me on my way. It wasn't as easy as I thought it would be. On the way home, I felt a little empty. I was quiet and didn't say anything to my friend. I was glad she was with me. James and I never talked about it; it was like it never happened. It started to bother me. Every time I saw a baby, I would feel sadness come over me. James didn't go with me, but he regretted it and that haunted him. Like I said, it was never spoken of, so life went on. It didn't stop us from having unprotected sex again.

James worked with a bunch of guys selling shirts at concerts. They did it illegally but made pretty good money. They would get chased by the cops at times. They would hold the shirts under their shirts and jackets. James got caught by the cops one time, and they beat him up. Then they took him back to the station. The captain took one look at James and all the bruises all over him, he told the officers to let him go. The captain knew his men shouldn't have beaten James up. I wonder if they ever got in trouble for that. James ran from the cops but never resisted when he got caught. I don't think that was the only time he got chased by cops. He did that for a few years I think. He also sold cocaine. He sold it for someone else. He got paid to do it, but he also used up some of his pay on the drugs. His mom found bags of it in the house and flushed it down the toilet. He told his mom he was going to get in trouble if he didn't give the man his money for all that cocaine she had just flushed down the toilet. He had to ask his sister-in-law for a loan to pay that man back. He had to pay her back by giving her a little money each week. He dropped out of school, and one of his brother's friends got him a job at a print shop. He now had a real paying job where no cops would be chasing him.

I went to a business school and used to see James in the morning on the train. We would ride together sometimes. I liked seeing him in the morning. I dropped out of school. My grandmother signed me out. My friend Regina was going to this business school and talked me into it. I took out a student loan to pay for the school and books. I wound up getting kicked out of it. I partied too much and didn't keep up my grades. I was disappointed, but it was my fault.

After a while, I just hung out with James and some other couples. We would continue to drink and hang out at the bars. The bars we hung out in weren't nice bars; they were dives! All my friends started doing cocaine, but I hadn't tried it yet. At a party, my friends were sitting in a circle and passing cocaine around for everybody to try. I was curious, wanted to know what everyone liked about it. I sat in the circle feeling a little nervous about trying it. I watched everybody else do it first so I would know what to do. When it was my turn, I starting shaking but then took the straw and snorted it up my nose. A few minutes later, I was buying my own bag. I loved the feeling it gave me. Cocaine made me talk more, stay up later, and drink more. It was like courage in a powdered form.

I continued to snort it every weekend. A friend of mine got me a job in the city, and she knew a dealer. We would walk to his office at lunchtime and snort cocaine with him. He would give us lines that were as large as buying a whole bag. I would go back to work high. It wasn't a high like smoking pot; you couldn't tell I was on it. James and I would do cocaine together. There were times I got it on my own and didn't tell James. I didn't want to share my cocaine; I wanted to last the whole night. James and I did lots of cocaine. We

50

would go in the bars' bathroom, roll up a dollar bill, or I would use my long pinky nail, and snort. When it came down to the last line, I would lick the paper it came in; it made my mouth numb, and I had to get every drop of it. I also liked the numbing sensation. I worked basically to get high every weekend. I did save enough to get to work on the train. (I worked for a ticket company. We made tickets for plays, sports, and other events.) One of the bars had a DJ, Hollywood Nights. On Saturday, we would go there because I loved to dance. Music took me to another place. It almost was like I was hypnotized. I would dance and sing in my bedroom. I would dance anywhere, even in the streets, if I heard music I liked. It was another escape I had from life, just like the drinking and the drugs. It made all my problems go away.

Chapter Thirteen

That is why a man leaves his father and mother and clings to his wife, and the two of them become one body. (Genesis 2:24)

Later, I found out I was pregnant again. This time we decided to keep the baby. We told James's mother; she wasn't happy but told us we had to get married, which was fine with me because I wanted to marry James anyway. I was nineteen and planning a fast and cheap wedding. I got laid off of my job and was worried about how we were going to live on one salary. James's mother always said that God will provide. My aunt Liza brought me a dress for $300. We got married in St. Thomas Church; even though I wasn't Catholic, the priest said he would marry us if I brought up my children Catholic. Uncle James walked me down the aisle. James's brother Jeremy was his best man. He told me later on that when I started up the aisle, James said, "She looks beautiful." I loved hearing that. My matron of honor was my sister-in-law, Karen. Karen and I were very close. We hung out with Karen and Leo a lot. We bought my mom a nice dress, and she looked great. The reception was at the Jewish war Veterans. We didn't send out invitations; it was just word of mouth. We couldn't pay for a photographer, so we asked a bartender that we knew to take some pictures because she had a good camera.

It wasn't the wedding of my dreams, but we had fun and so did everyone else. The day of the wedding, our photographer was sick. I was very disappointed. Everybody who had a camera gave us some pictures, but they weren't of the greatest quality. My mother was so funny; she walked in with my uncle James on her arm. She had her hand up in the air waving it around and yelling out something, like she was the center of attraction. She looked so happy and had a great time that night. A lot of people showed up for the wedding. One of the girls I used to work with gave us cocaine for a wedding present instead of money. I drank beer and snorted that night. It was a regret I would have the rest of my life. I was about five months pregnant. We had a great time. We found out there was a fight at the end of the reception with some family members. There was always some drama going on. When the reception was over, we went to after hours and my dress got trashed. The bottom of my dress was black from everyone stepping on it at after hours. On our wedding night, friends of ours let us use their apartment; they stayed at someone else's house. We didn't have money for a hotel. We didn't have anywhere to live. We had to live with James's mother and father for a while. The only thing we bought with our wedding money was a TV. We had to pay the DJ with some of the money we took out of the envelopes we got that night. Thinking we used the rest on drugs.

We finally found an apartment in his mother's apartment building. Our first apartment had only three rooms: one bedroom, living room, and kitchen. We had no money to buy furniture, so his boss gave us some of his furniture that he didn't want anymore. My grandmother brought us our first bedroom set, and she got me a little washing machine so I wouldn't have to go down a flight of stairs with laundry. I was pregnant, and she was afraid I would fall down the stairs. We had wood floors in the living room, but they were all worn out, so we painted the floor brown.

I gave birth to James Jr. that April. We were at James's brother's house for a communion party. I was eating tons of salami, one of my cravings. We lived right around the corner, so we walked home. James wanted to go to the bar. I told him no. I was already two weeks late. I could go into labor any time now. He was a little mad, but he came home with me. We went to bed, and then the contractions started. The contractions came every three minutes from the beginning. We called James's brother Bob, and he picked us up. I went to the hospital; my sister-in-law Karen met us there. Karen came in the room with us. She was wiping sweat off of James's forehead; he was so nervous he was dripping sweat on me. I gave birth to my son five hours later. I was twenty years old, and James was twenty-one. The doctor pointed out that he had an extra thumb, and we both blamed ourselves for that. We were both drinking and doing drugs when he was conceived and me a few times after I knew I was pregnant. The doctor said we could remove it when he was one year old, and that's what we did.

He was such a good baby. He slept through the night after two weeks. That was because my mother-in-law told me to give him cereal in the bottle at night. As he got older, we discovered that he had a learning disability and ADHD. It wasn't easy, especially being so young. James's mom was so good with James Jr. My mother-in-law had a bad back, but that didn't stop her from playing on the floor with him. And she always had Kit-Kats and peanut butter cups in the refrigerator for him. She was a great grandmother. All her grandkids called her Nanny.

My mother was now living by herself and going out in the middle of the night for cigarettes. James's mother said she needed to be taken care of. We were just married and didn't want the responsibility. I had to take her to the county hospital, and they would find her a place to live. That day was very hard for me. I was so upset leaving her there, but I knew she would be safe.

James was still going out on the weekends unless we had friends over the house. He would stay out until morning, and that would piss me off. I wasn't mad at him for going out drinking but because he was out without me. I was still young and wanted to party too. After a while, it was getting too much for me. I would call all the bars to see which one he was in. He would tell anybody who picked up the phone that he wasn't there. (Later on, James confessed, after he had stopped drinking.) He wanted to stop drinking but wasn't very successful.

We decided to move away, thinking that would stop James from drinking, but that didn't work either. James would just drive back to the old neighborhood. I would go back to the old neighborhood too. I would go visit Linda. She had been married before me and had two beautiful children. I didn't see Sissy that much anymore. We lost track of some of our friends. We all went in different directions.

I had a twenty-fifth birthday party at my house for James and decided to invite some of the old friends. It was great seeing a lot of these people. James and one of his friends took a ride while the party was still going and went to buy some cocaine, but I didn't know about it at that time. Everybody had a good time. That might have been the last time we hung out with all of them.

Yet again, my grandmother made me feel bad. Liza had a baby boy named Donny. He wound up being very smart too, just like Charlene. All I heard was how smart they both were. She would brag about them to everyone. But was I ever in the conversation? No. Did she brag about my son? No. it really hurt me. I felt like I was invisible. She always used to tell me I should take classes in college. I always told her I was fine being a mother and wife. She thought I should have a career and be someone who was smart and made a lot of money. It didn't make me feel good about myself. I know she didn't mean to hurt me, but nevertheless, it hurt.

I still did a lot of stupid things after I got married. I had gotten my permit, not my license yet. I would pick up my friend Lauren and drive her around when James was at work. I was trying to park the car and hit the car in front of me. Lauren and I looked at each other and said let's get out of here. I never did tell James about that. I wasn't allowed to be driving without a licensed driver. Another time, I was out with Lauren shopping and I was supposed to be watching her son and I lost him! We were looking all over for him, and he was hiding under a rack of clothes. Lauren and I loved going shopping together. I spent a lot of time with Lauren when James Jr. was a baby. We grew apart, but later in life, we reconnected. I'm happy to have her back in my life.

Chapter Fourteen

Hear, my son, your father's instruction, and reject
not your mother's teaching. (Proverbs 1:8)

James's mom, Mary, was a wonderful woman. I always loved talking to her. She had a good sense of humor and was very loving. She would talk to me about her faith, and I was always interested in what she had to say. My family was Jewish, but we didn't practice it. I would ask her questions about Jesus. She would pray a rosary every day. She told me I would convert and become Catholic one day. She was like a mother to me. She really took me under her wings. She was always there when I needed her. She was the most generous and kind woman I have ever met. And she always told it like it was, very honest. James's father, Bob, was very quiet. He used to let my son James Jr. sit on his lap and color with him. He even sang to him a couple of times. James's father was old school; he would come home from work and sit in his chair. James's mother did everything for her husband and her children.

I loved James's family. James had four brothers: Bob, Tim, Leo, and Jeremy. The family was close to each other, and I liked that about them. They always got together once a week for dinner and always celebrated everyone's birthday, no matter how old they were. The family wasn't prefect, but they were perfect for me. We spent a lot of time with the family. There were so many birthday parties, baptisms, communions, confirmations, and so forth. There was always something going on in the family. Aunt Liza didn't like that I spent so much time with them and not my family. But I had so many bad memories of my family life. It was just easier to stay away. It wasn't that I didn't love them. I just hated all the drama and yelling that went on every time my family got together. My aunt thought that it was James who kept me away from my family, but that wasn't the case; it was me who stayed away. Every time my family would come over, I would be a nervous wreck. It would put me in a bad mood, and then it would cause problems for James and me. We would always have a fight when my family came over. My stomach would be in knots. My grandmother would yell at my mother. Liza would yell at my grandmother. My mother would yell at both of them. So much chaos, my head would spin.

James and I moved again. James was doing a lot of overtime, and we were able to buy some new furniture. I was very excited about that. James's brother went to an AA meeting and told him about it. We were a little shocked by that news. We didn't think he had a problem. It took a little while, but then James started to go the meetings.

James was doing very well with the AA meetings, but I wasn't. I was a little jealous he had somewhere to go every night and new friends. We were having problems. I told him twice that I didn't think I was in love with him anymore. He was devastated; he couldn't understand why I would feel this way, especially since he had stopped drinking. I realized I didn't know what love was. I didn't have any good married role models. I wasn't being intimate with James. I didn't have the same feelings that I used to, and sex made me feel dirty.

I went to see a therapist. She told me that I didn't like sex because my uncle sexually abused me. It was one of my big crosses I had to carry. At times I thought it would be easier to be on my own so I wouldn't have to worry about having sex with my husband. I went to a support group twice but didn't feel comfortable talking to strangers about my love life. So I decided to suffer alone. It was me and my miserable self. I was my worst enemy.

The therapist I saw wasn't giving me helpful advice. She told me that in order to have a better sex life, I should watch porn. She also told me to write a letter to the uncle that molested me because he had passed away and I had no closure. I wrote a letter, but it did nothing for me. There was no closure. I stopped seeing that therapist and things did start to get a little better between James and me, in spite of the bad therapist.

I started a new job in the city, but it didn't last long. My son James Jr. got kicked out of preschool. He had special needs that they couldn't handle. He would cry a lot and had to be held all the time. They had too many other kids that needed to be taken care of too. They didn't have the time to give him all the attention. I had to become a stay-at-home mom. I didn't have much confidence in myself. I didn't finish high school and flunked out at business school. I felt stupid and useless.

I became friends with some of James's AA friends and would go to the open meetings. One of my good friends started going with James to the meetings. After the opened meetings, we would go to the diner to hang out. I started to like being with his friends and their girlfriends or wives. I felt a part of something again. I didn't feel so alone anymore.

We had another baby, this one was planned. With this pregnancy, I did things a lot different. I had smoked and drank with James Jr. I also ate everything I wanted. I gained forty-two pounds with James Jr. This time I ate so heathy, and there was no smoking or drinking. I only gained twenty-five pounds with this pregnancy. James Jr. was only six pounds and eleven and a half ounces. The weight was all mine with him. At the age of twenty-seven, I gave birth to a beautiful little girl named Danielle. She was nine pounds and fifteen ounces. She was a big girl. She was and still is beautiful. Her hair looked dark at first, but then she got this beautiful red head of hair with little curls in the back. She would twirl her hair even as an infant. Her big brother, James Jr., loved her. We were so happy. We had a boy and a girl. They were seven years apart. I was done with having kids. I just wanted two children. Or so I thought.

Life seemed better but still hard. It would continue to be hard as long as I had to make love to James. There were times when I felt sexy and in the mood, and then sex would be great for a couple of weeks. But it never lasted. Then I would think too much and set myself up for failure, and sex was then bad again. I would feel like I was being raped at times. I was still not much of a talker and couldn't talk about feelings. I didn't have the tools to cope with it. I also thought if I told him I didn't like sex, he would blame it on himself, and I couldn't hurt him like that. It was not James's fault. I never said anything to him at that time. Later on in our marriage, I told him about my uncle, and then he understood. A certain way he kissed me, the way he would rub up against me, would bring back all the horrible memories of Hank. It killed me that I felt that way. I wanted to be able to make love to my husband. I started to get depressed. I had to be put on medication.

James got a new job in the Union. He was doing air condition and heating. He did a lot of overtime so we could have money. He was moving up from helper to a mechanic. James quickly moved up the ladder at work. He was good at his job, and lots of people liked James. He is a great people person, and that got him far. James is a smart man too. He wanted to keep learning. He took lots of classes through the Union.

When Danielle was two years old, we moved to New Jersey. Things were still kind of tough on me. Intimacy was still an issue. But I loved being in Jersey, and I love my house. It was also great living close to my brother-in-law, sister-in-law, Bob and Regina, and their seven kids. We would go to their house for all the kids' birthdays and stay over. It was about an hour to get home, and there was always lots of traffic. Their house would have people all over, after a party, on couches and floors. It was great being with them. Every one of the kids in the family loved going to their aunt Regina's house. They would all cry when they had to leave. James's other brother Tim and Doreen also lived in Jersey. They had a daughter the same age as my daughter. They were close when they were young. Tim also had a son a little younger than James Jr. There were lots of cousins in the family. Later on, his other brother Jeremy and his wife Liz moved to Hazlet. It was only ten minutes away. They had four kids. So now most of the family was in New Jersey. His brother Leo remarried a wonderful woman named Lily. They liked Brooklyn and stayed there. Leo had two kids with his first wife Karen and had one kid with Lily. It was a large family!

We lived in a townhouse that had four levels. We had come from a three-room apartment, so this townhouse was like a mansion to us. We were able to buy new furniture. James had a good job and would work overtime so we could have more things. We were able to get a van for me, so I wouldn't have to be stuck in the house. Things got a little better. We met some new friends in Jersey, plus almost all of his brothers were in New Jersey now. James's mother and father came to Jersey to live with James's oldest brother and his family. It was nice to be close to the family. Jersey was so clean and country-like compared to Brooklyn. I liked it. Especially having a house, that didn't even cross my mind that we would ever own a house. We had a dining room; that was like a big deal! Kids had their own room. It was great! We had a little backyard but a lot of common space that anyone could use. There was a park across the way and tennis courts, which I never used. We could walk to QuickChek when we needed milk or anything else we wanted there. My daughter made friends with a cute little girl; her family lived in the back of our house. Our backyard opened to the front of her house. And I became good friends with her mother.

I always liked to surprise James with nice things for his birthday. Especially things he wouldn't think of me getting him. Some were tickets to a Broadway play. Once it was a weekend away, without the kids. But the best one of all was a truck. We had looked at a truck he liked, but he wasn't ready to get it. James took forever to buy cars. It drove me a little crazy at times. A friend of ours had known someone in the dealership that could give us a special price for it. I wanted him to have that truck, so I went back to the dealership while James was at work and bought the truck. I decided to surprise him in a special way. He used to park his car at the bus depot. I had an extra key. I moved his car out of his spot and put the truck in that spot. I also took a hat that was in his car that he would recognize and put it on the dashboard. We waited and hid from him. When he got off the bus, he was with a friend, and he was looking for his car. We could hear him saying to his friend, "I know I parked the car here. This truck looks like the one I wanted to buy," and then he looked at the hat and said, "That's my hat!" He looked so confused and continued to look around for his car. He said, "What is going on here?" My friend and I jumped out and said, "Surprise!" His friend started to laugh, and he was very surprised! That was so much fun watching his face. He was like, "Are you serious? This is my truck?" I said, "Yes, it is."

James surprised me one day. He took me to a play in the city for my thirtieth birthday, and when we got home, I saw our curtain move. I thought there was someone in our house. I was scared. He said he would go in and check. I told him not to go in the house, but he did. Then he came out and said to come in, that it was fine. I went in slowly and scared and then, I was surprised by a bunch of friends yelling out "Happy birthday!" Another time, we went to Florida, and while we were there, he told me he had a surprise for me. He took me to swim with the dolphins! I told him a while ago that I always wanted to swim with dolphins. It was great! I loved it so much. Then I had a sea lion kiss me on my face. I loved that too. That was a great trip.

Not too long after that, James's mom passed away. It was devastating to us all. Everyone in the family had a wonderful relationship with her; she was one of a kind. I still think of her often. A year after that, James's father passed away. Even though he was sick as well, he probably died from a broken heart. James's parents had been together for a very long time. James had lost both his parents in one year. It was a terrible loss. It was hard on the family to lose such wonderful parents, grandmother and grandfather, and mother and father-in-law. It was like losing a part of yourself. But we stuck together because James's parents would have hated her family to fall apart. They made sure they still did things as a family. James's mother made such an impact on me and the whole family. We have a great family because of her and all the prayers she said for the family. I believe she is still praying for her family but now in a better place.

At our townhouse, our neighbors were drinking in front of their house (which was attached to our house) and cursing. One Halloween, we all got dressed up to go trick or treating, even James got in a costume. Boys and girls from the neighborhood started throwing eggs at the children. James and a friend ran after them. It was a little funny because his friend was in a lion costume and James was in a rabbit costume chasing these kids. The cops wound up coming, and the kids were so disrespectful, they didn't even care how they talked to the cops. The girls had worse language than the boys. We had little kids and had to bring them in the house so they didn't hear the language. Our next-door neighbor's kids would hang out in the front of the house with their friends; they were very disrespectful. The girls would curse their own mother out. We moved out of Brooklyn to get away from this stuff.

We became friends with some of our other neighbors, but it was time to get our own house that wasn't attached to anyone else's. We moved not far from where we were living, maybe ten minutes away by car. The kids were in school, and James decided to get his GED. We both didn't finish high school. After he got his GED, I decided to get mine. I went to classes once a week, and the teacher told me when I was ready to take the test. I was so nervous because when I was a little younger, I tried to take that test without studying and failed. I was so happy that I passed the test. I even went to a small graduation ceremony. My family went as well, and as I walked up to receive my diploma, I felt proud. Danielle said that she was very proud of me. I finally felt like I accomplished something. After that, I eventually got bored and needed something else to do. I got a job at Costco in the bakery section. I gained a little weight with that job. I would do overnights for the holidays to get all the pies out. If the baked goods were broken, we were allowed to eat them. Yummy! Later I decided to take a test to get a license to drive a school bus. I got a job, and I was able to take my kids to school. I drove a mini school bus for a few years. It helped me get over a fear of getting lost, and I learned how to read a map.

Chapter Fifteen

When you stand to pray, forgive anyone against whom you have a grievance, so that your heavenly Father may in turn forgive your transgressions. (Mark 11:25)

My aunt Liza decided that she wanted to try and find my mother's firstborn, my brother which she had given away years ago. We didn't know who adopted him and thought it would take a long time to find him. My aunt Liza worked as a school secretary and had ways of looking up other schools. She typed in my brother's name and found out where he was; he went to school not that far from where we lived. She found him through his given name. Unfortunately, he had never been adopted. She found out the name and address of his last foster family. She contacted them and asked where he was. They told us he had finished school and enlisted into the army. He then was discharged because he had a mental breakdown.

We found out he was living in Ohio, and James and I decided to take a car trip to see him. The trip was long, and it was snowing. We stayed in a hotel for a night and started driving again in the morning. When we got to his apartment, he gave us a hug. He was physically a little man; my whole family was little. Anthony was a very thin man with brown hair. He reminded me of my cousin Carl. He kept on calling me "Sis," which made me a little uncomfortable. After all, we were strangers really. This was the first time ever meeting me. We took him out for lunch, and he prayed. He said he was a Christian, and he could quote many Bible verses. He told us he was married but now divorced and had a set of twin girls. He showed me their picture; they were identical and very cute. His girls lived with his ex-wife's mother. The twin's mother was on drugs and couldn't take care of them. He now worked in a grocery store. It was time to go home, and we said our good-byes.

Anthony would call me and leave messages like, "Hi, Sis, I miss you and I love you." I didn't feel very comfortable with that. He was still a stranger to me. But the rest of the family opened their arms to him, sending him money and talking to him as if they knew him all their lives. Anthony got married again, and he wanted us to meet his new wife and their son. He decided to take a trip to New York. I told my aunt and grandmother he can come to my house to visit but he can't stay over. He stayed at Liza's house.

Months later, his wife called my aunt, telling her he was abusive and he would watch porn on their computer. He also got fired from his job for sexual harassment. He continued to call me "Sis" and tell me that he loved me. I told my aunt that I wasn't comfortable with it, and she wound up telling him. I felt so betrayed; she had known me all my life and only met him twice. I got in a big argument on the phone with her, and I began cursing her out. She told me James had me in a plastic bubble and was controlling me, but to me, she was the one who always was controlling. That was it for me. I stopped talking to her.

My grandmother wasn't happy with me not talking to Liza, but I stopped inviting her to get-togethers. I told my grandmother that I would pray for her, but I couldn't have anything to do with her for a while. It would get me physically ill thinking about it. Every time my family came to my house, James and I would fight. I would be a wreck being with them. There was always screaming when they were at my house, and Grandma would always yell at my mom to stop talking to herself. There was no peace in the house when all of them were over. We didn't talk for years, but I eventually felt God heal me from that hurt, and I decided to forgive her. Now if my brother texts me, I try to text him back, although I still really don't know him very well. My mother was so happy that we found him. She used to ask me, "Did you call your brother?" I would tell her no, in a nasty and disrespectful way. I really should have said, "He's all right, you don't have to worry about him." It would have made her feel better. I would let her call him from my house sometimes. It really was a big thing that she had her son back, even if she only saw him a few times. I should have let her talk to him more.

One of those crazy family days, my aunt Sheila and her daughter went to the store to pick up some soda, I think. It was a calm day, but when they got back, Sheila was screaming and cursing her daughter out. I had to bring the kids in the other room because of all the bad language that was being said. I was told it all happened because her daughter told her she went the wrong way. Sheila freaked out. She grabbed her pocketbook and walked out the door. That was the last time Sheila was in my house. I believe she was mentally ill and needed help. One day we were meeting the family in Brooklyn for dinner in a restaurant in Sheepshead Bay, when we saw my cousin Charlene walking down the street by herself. She was young, not old enough to be on her own. She told us she had a fight with her mom (Aunt Sheila) and her mom told her to take a bus to the restaurant. Sheila still came in her car and made her little girl go by herself. We all argued with her on the way in the restaurant. Sheila's mouth was so foul; she talked worse than a truck driver. (I don't know where the saying came from. I'm sure not all truck drivers spoke like that.) The words that came out of Sheila's mouth were disgusting. I wasn't a saint and used bad language too, but she was gross.

My cousin wound up living with my grandmother. My cousin went through a lot of crap but came out on top. She didn't let it stop her from being a straight-A student and graduating from Columbia University in NYC. Then moving on to medical school and becoming a doctor. I'm so proud of her. But I was a little envious too. She was so smart, she could have been anything she wanted to be. I wanted to be as smart as she was, and I wanted a career too. I let my fears get in the way of that. I put it in my head that I couldn't do it.

In 1998, I decided that I wanted to join the Catholic Church. I started to go to adult classes so that I could get baptized and confirmed. During this time, I also decided that I did not want to have any more children, and so I decided to have my tubes surgically tied. I wanted to be free. My kids were getting older, and I had more freedom. I knew that teachings of the Catholic Church did not coincide with this procedure, but I decided to have it done anyway. I thought if I did it before I became Catholic, it wouldn't count as a sin. The things we can talk ourselves into when we really want something, I was trying to justify what I was doing. I was even proud to say I had my tubes tied to others. It was me trying to feel okay with what I did. But I did like having more freedom, and I didn't think I could handle another child.

On Easter of 1999, I became a member of the Catholic Church. My cousin Charlene was also baptized on the same day but at a different church, St. Patrick's Cathedral in New York. The Mass was beautiful, even though it was done in the school's gym. There were so many people in our parish that the church was too small to fit everybody. So Mass was in the school gym. We would call it Our Lady of the Courts because that was where the basketball court was. I felt my mother-in-law's presence, as if she was rooting me on. James felt her there too. I asked my sister-in-law Doreen to be my sponsor. A few people said, "Now you'll feel the guilt." I thought that was funny. We had a small party after at our house.

Not long after that, Danielle received her First Holy Communion. We were all receiving Jesus now. It was very nice to be in church with James's family. I loved having a large family. They were and still are very close to one another. James's mother had a lot to do with that. Family was very important to her. After her passing, to keep the family still close, the whole family would go on vacation every other year. We went to Lake George, New York. The family got bigger and bigger. It was a great vacation. We would take turns cooking. Everyone had to cook just one night; the other nights were free nights. We continue to go there every other year, and I always look forward to that week with the family.

We also started our own tradition, going to the Thanksgiving Parade every year. We started that tradition when Danielle was two years old and James Jr. was nine years old. We would stay in New York City the night before, go to a movie, dinner, and walk around. It was fun, but I was always freezing. We had to get up very early in the morning to get a spot up front for the kids to see. We would wait for hours till the parade would start. Bathroom breaks were hard. And our hands and feet would get numb.

The second year we went to the parade, other family members came with us. We decided to go ice staking the night before. We were with James's oldest brother and his family. I didn't get on the ice, but James thought he should try and the kids went. It was in Central Park. James Jr. did okay at it, and Danielle had to have a little help from her cousins. They were all having fun. Then I saw James on the ice, he fell. One of the kids said they heard a crack. He was in a lot of pain. He couldn't get up, so they called an ambulance and it came and drove right on the ice. I got in it with him and my sister and brother-in-law said they would watch the kids for us. We were in the hospital for hours. He broke his ankle in two places. They put a cast on his foot and halfway up his leg. We wound up still going to the parade in his cast and crutches. That was the first and the last time James would try to skate. After many years of staying outside for the parade, and freezing our buns off, he got us a stop in a building. Now it's warm and the kids can run around and watch the parade. And best of all, there is a bathroom.

Chapter Sixteen

Jesus spoke to them again, saying "I am the light of the world. Whoever follows me will not walk in darkness, but will have the light of life." (John 8:12)

Danielle started to have nightmares about us killing her. She started to sleepwalk and didn't remember getting up and talking to me. Then her skin issues began, and clothes were starting to hurt her. She would scream as she would pull all her clothes off. That was a very hard time. It wasn't easy to get her out of the house while she was crying and pulling her clothes off. I didn't know what was going on. I saw a show on TV about OCD, and one of the kids was doing the same things with her clothes. We had to buy her clothes that were two sizes bigger, so she would keep them on. I researched it a little more and found out she had a sensory processing disorder. We took her to a therapist and they suggested rolling a round rubber brush on her body a few times a day. They said that would help her, but it didn't. They told me she needed to be disciplined because she was acting out negatively toward them, which she was, but I felt as though they were being rude about it. After all, she was a child that was suffering from some issues. I was really upset with them and might have been a little rude to them back.

Soon we started going to these prayer meetings that were held at our local parish. The meetings were weird to us at the beginning; they spoke in tongues, which sounded crazy. We thought they were looney, but we liked the praise and worship music. We kept on going and started to like it all. We learned a lot about our faith, especially about the devil and his tricks. I was given a book called the *Miracle*

Hour and started reading and praying the part about spiritual warfare. I prayed it every night for Danielle. It was a miracle; Danielle's bad dreams stopped, and her sensitivity to clothes went away! What a blessing it was to see Danielle wearing clothes her size without them hurting her. God was healing my baby girl. That proved to me she was getting attacked by the devil. We met another family in the community that had a daughter with the same clothes issue; we told them to do the spiritual warfare prayers. It worked for them too. We began to love the meetings and the people who were there. We became close to many families. We were getting closer to God. We became close to the priest who was in charge of the prayer meeting. I also as a mother wanted a better life for my kids than I had. I realized faith was very important; you aren't alone. There is a way out. Hope! I saw how James's mother lived; her faith united the whole family in good times and bad.

One day, a friend from my prayer meetings asked me out to lunch. We sat down at the diner and opened our menus; something fell out of mine. I looked at it and saw it was a medal. On the medal was St. Padre Pio. His face was on a rounded bubble-like thing on top of a metal round charm. We asked the waitress if someone left it behind. She didn't know, but she told me to keep it. I held on to it and then started to wear it on my chain. I never really thought of him before. I knew he had the stigmata (the marks of Jesus on his hands) and he would bleed from his hands. He also had the gift of knowing people's sins before they told him. I thought that was cool.

One day, I was at a restaurant with a few families, and I touched my Padre Pio medal. I didn't feel the bubble on it, the picture of St. Padre Pio was gone. I looked under the table and on the floor around us but didn't see it. I went to the bathroom thinking maybe it fell off in there. I looked all over the bathroom. I was upset. I looked at the medal in the mirror and saw something on it. It was very small, but when I looked closer, it was a picture of Our Lady of Czestochowa, the Black Madonna. I couldn't believe there was a picture behind another picture. I found that to be strange. Why would they do that? Nobody would know it's there unless the first picture came off. I said it has to be a sign. Maybe he is telling me to take everything to the blessed mother. I never thought about Mary too much. I started to ask Mother Mary to talk to her son for me. He would listen to her. I wound up putting the medal away and then someone gave me the same medal. I never tried to take the picture off this one. So I say St. Padre Pio came to me. He guided me to the Blessed Mother. Many years later, someone gave me a rosary with Padre Pio on it and all the mysteries had all the images of the Blessed Mother on both sides. He is pushing me to say the rosary now.

Chapter Seventeen

He will cover you with his feathers, and under his wings you will find refuge; his faithfulness will be your shield and rampart. You will not fear the terror of the night, nor the arrow that flies by day, nor the pestilence that stalks in the darkness, nor the plague that destroys at midday. A thousand may fall at your side, ten thousand at your right hand, but it will not come near you. (Psalm 91:4–7)

The next year, James and I decided that we wanted to homeschool our children. There were others in the community that homeschooled as well. When James first asked me about it, I was very against it. I wasn't good in school; how could I ever teach my kids at home? There were things going on in school that I didn't want my kids to learn. We wanted them to grow up without the influences of the world. We wanted holy kids, not worldly kids. So I prayed and also went to a friend's house, Darlene, to see her homeschooling books. She said wonderful things about it. She said I would have all the answer keys for all the work, which made me feel a lot better.

So I ordered the books and took my kids out of school. At first I was just going to homeschool Danielle because my son James Jr. was in Special Education. I didn't think I could teach him. But one day, he came home from school and he put on a long-sleeved shirt and it was very hot that day. I saw something sticking out of his sleeve, and I asked him what it was. He said nothing. I thought it was a little suspicious, and I pulled his sleeve up. There was a big bandage around his arm. I asked him what happened; it took a while to get it out of him, but then he told me everything. He was in his first year of high school, the boys were making fun of his size, and they would lock him out of the changing room before or after soccer. He thought if he carved his name with a paper clip on his arm he would look cool. But then he got mad, and after carving his name on his arm, he then started to carve it out. There were carving marks all over his arms. That was it for me; he was not going back to that school. I took him out and started homeschooling both kids. I called the homeschool group where I got the books from. Told them he was in Special Ed. They sent him a test to see what level he was at. They sent him special books. We would meet once a week with the other homeschoolers so that our children would be able to get together and socialize. I was very happy with our decision. The kids liked it too, at least at first. Later on, Danielle wanted to go back to school. It was a life saver for James Jr.

After a while of homeschooling, Danielle was rebelling some. She would tell me, "I don't have to believe in God just because you do." We made lots of mistakes in our early conversion. So I asked Mother Mary to please show Danielle her son and show her the truth. It didn't take that long before I saw a difference in her. I didn't say a word, just kept praying to the Blessed Mother. I told the Blessed Mother to take over. She started to show an interest in the faith by asking us questions about Mary. That is when I really started to have a devotion to the Blessed Mary. She was showing me how to be a better mother. I had a long way to go myself. I wasn't the mother I wanted to be. I think it's going to be a lifelong lesson. I could never be the perfect mother that she was, but I could strive for it. I was new to the religion and needed to get closer to God myself. I would just have to show her without words. Be the best I could be and, when I fall, make sure I say I'm sorry. Showing her I wasn't perfect but that was okay, nobody was. Showing her I could forgive even when I really didn't want to, but I knew in my heart it was the right thing to do. She saw her parents try to live a good life and teach her and James Jr. that God and we would love both of them no matter what.

When I was thinking about homeschooling, before we made the final decision, I was in the Adoration Chapel praying for an answer. It was very quiet in the chapel, so peaceful. I wanted so much for

Jesus to speak to me. I wasn't a good listener; my mind would wander from one thing to another, and I could never concentrate. I decided to listen to my breathing so I wouldn't be thinking of anything. All of a sudden, I heard a voice tell me to stop driving a school bus (I was a school bus driver for a few years) and homeschool my children. It shocked me, and I looked around to see who it was. Nobody was in the room but me and Jesus. I couldn't believe it! Jesus spoke to me. I started to laugh with excitement. Of course I tried that breathing again but nothing else happened. It was a little funny because I started breathing so hard I started to bring attention to myself. By then, there were more people in the chapel, and they were looking at me. One of them might have asked if I was okay, and with a big smile on my face, I told them I was fine. I never did hear Jesus like that again. There were other ways he would speak to me, through friends, priests, and the scripture.

Chapter Eighteen

Our mouths were filled with laughter; our tongues sang for joy. Then it was said among the nation, "The Lord has done great things for them." The Lord has done great things for us; oh, how happy we were! (Psalm 126:2–3)

Another time that I experienced God was during a healing mass. I started to smile and couldn't stop. I believe that the Holy Spirit gave me a gift of smiling or happiness. I was at a retreat when we were praying for the Holy Spirit to come upon us when I looked up and saw a dove! I was so excited! I was on a God high for a while, but there were some things that bothered me about the community that we were now a part of. I didn't like some of the things that the people were saying. I had to dress a certain way and stop watching television shows that I liked, and I did that for a while but I started to feel like a Stepford wife. I felt, at times, put down for not agreeing with some of the women in the community. James was definitely more into it than I was. I thought everything I did was wrong and started to act more like them, but in the process, I became very judgmental. I started thinking I was better than everyone who didn't act the way we did. It led to me pushing myself away from some people. I pushed away some family members too. Something I wasn't very proud of. We are not supposed to be judging others. And yet I felt judged too by other so-called religious people.

We changed our family life dramatically. I threw out all my Disney movies and made the kids stop watching shows that we now thought were inappropriate. Everything had to be rated G or PG. I changed the way I dressed and the way the kids dressed. I started dressing like an old lady, and that wasn't me. It was too much at once. No wonder my daughter turned away from the church. We did a lot of things wrong, but we also did a lot of things right.

Don't get me wrong, the community did a lot for me and my family. We were definitely heading in the right direction. I loved our charismatic Mass and the praise and worship. It brought me closer to God. The community was going through a lot of changes; it made some mistakes, but for the most part, it was a good place to be. The community had to do some growing up, like a child making mistakes in the beginning because the child is too young to make the right decisions. The community had to get older and learn by its mistakes.

The closer I got to God, the more attacked I got by the devil. One night in bed, I saw a shadow outside my bedroom door. I felt evil there, and I started to call on the name of Jesus. It was there for a few minutes, then it left. I remember watching a Veggie Tales movie, God is bigger than the boogeyman, with the kids. Trying to remember if I called on the name of Jesus, Satan would flee. I never felt evil like that again in my house. I decided to have the house blessed by Father King. Father King is a great priest and friend. The devil knew all my weaknesses and preyed on them. I would ask Father King to pray over me very often.

I loved when we would go to Florida with Father King and some other families in the community. We would have Mass every day in Father King's villa. We would do a lot of things with the community. We went to different shrines, went to the Outer Banks a few times, and a nice hotel in Pennsylvania. Father King's favorite place was Florida because he loved palm trees and sun. I loved it too. We had Lord's Day Suppers and healing Masses. It was great because there were a lot of families together and a lot of other children for my children to play with. If it wasn't for the community, I wouldn't have wanted more children. I felt God put it on my heart to have more children, and I had a great desire for them. God was changing me so much. There were big families in the community, and I wanted to be one of them. But there was a problem because I had my tubes tied before I became Catholic and because of that could not conceive. Before my conversion, I didn't think I could handle more children, like I would go crazy. But I had a feeling that God was changing me to be able to handle it.

I told James to sit on the bed; I needed to talk to him. James looked nervous, like, "What is she about to tell me?" I told him I wanted to reverse my tubal ligation and wanted more children. He was very surprised to hear I wanted more children. I think he was relieved that I wasn't leaving him. He said we should pray about it first. We prayed about it and decided to have the reversal procedure done. I went through with the procedure and the doctor said it would be very hard to get pregnant because my tubes were clogged. We tried for a while but nothing happened. I was very disappointed. I really wanted another child, so I surprised James again by asking him if we could adopt. After some prayer, we decided to talk to a family that adopted from South Korea. We decided to use the same agency they did. Wow, there was a lot of paperwork to do for this adoption! We were very excited! It took us fourteen months from start to finish. When we got his picture, we already were in love with him. The picture showed him at a couple of days old. He was so adorable. I couldn't wait to hold him. Our two children were very excited too. I was thirty-eight years old when we were blessed with our third child.

The adoption agency had an escort bring our new baby boy to us, and we waited at the airport for him. We had some family and friends with us. We were all so excited! It seemed like we were waiting forever. Then we saw on the board the plane had landed. But we had to wait some more. The longer I waited, the more nervous I got. We had to wait till everyone else got off the plane before all the babies would come out. They told us to wait until we heard our names called, and then we could take him. I was so nervous; I couldn't believe this was happening. They all started coming out, I felt like I couldn't stop shaking, my heart was beating so hard, and then we heard our names called. We went over to the man holding our son Andrew Kim; the man put him straight in my arms. He was so cute, and he smelled so good. This beautiful boy was now in my arms. James and I were in tears. We were so happy.

We named him after the Saint Andrew Kim Taegon, who was the first Catholic priest in South Korea. He was martyred with another priest and a hundred other people for their faith. Andrew's name in Korea had the name Kim in it, so I thought it would be a perfect name for him. We took him home and stared at him for a while. He was a good baby. Andrew was six months old when we got him. My daughter, Danielle, couldn't stop staring at his little feet. Soon as we got home, she took off his socks. Some of our friends had left a big sign in the window, welcoming him home. It was a wonderful day! He adjusted to us quickly. We were all very happy to have a baby in the house again. The first few weeks, we had family and friends come visit our new son.

Chapter Nineteen

Have no anxiety at all, but in everything, by prayer and petition, with thanksgiving, make your request known to God. Then the peace of God that surpasses all understanding will guard your heart and minds in Christ Jesus. (Philippians 4:6–7)

A few months after he came home to us, I was shopping with my daughter when I got a call from James. He said to come right home because Andrew needed me. I was a little upset that he couldn't take care of him for a little while, while we finished up our shopping. When I got home, James was upset. He saw Andrew have a seizure. It happened again while I was home. We took him to a doctor and found out he had a febrile seizure, which meant that he gets seizures when he has a fever. He had many of them; the seizures were very scary to see. He wouldn't move after having one. We would just turn him to his side and talk to him until he came out of it. Many times I would cry and pray. The doctor said he would grow out of them when he turned seven.

He had one in the ocean once and didn't have a fever. It was very hot that day, and my friend Dena and I went to the beach. Dena was in the water with Andrew when it happened. They were holding hands and jumping over the waves and Andrew would go under the water. This time when he went under, he took a little longer to get up and his hand was feeling weird. She pulled him up and yelled to me. He was limp and unresponsive. There was something wrong. I ran to her, and we placed him on the sand on his side. A nurse happened to be there, so she came to help. I told her about his seizures. The lifeguard brought a truck on the sand and took us to their first-aid office. We put him in a bed and waited for him to wake up. The lifeguards wanted to call an ambulance, but I have been through this many times already. The lifeguard scared me when they said that if he drank a lot of the saltwater, it could hurt him. So we went to the hospital. He was checked out and sent home. We were very pleased to hear that there wasn't anything wrong with his lungs. Another time, we were in North Carolina with another family, renting a beautiful big house together. We were in a hot tub, and then the kids went into a very cold pool. Andrew had a seizure from the hot tub to the pool; he looked like he was going to fall asleep in the pool. I yelled to James to get him. I think Andrew did say he was tired right before that. Then again that same day in the ocean it happened. We discovered that he didn't need to have a fever; it was his body temperature going down too quickly that did it. That was very scary; he could have drowned if we weren't there. I was very careful to watch him every time he went into a pool.

He was getting older, and I was scared the seizures would occur at school. I wasn't worried for nothing because he had a seizure in preschool. They called an ambulance, and by the time I got there, they had him on oxygen. He started to come out of it, and I told them I would take him home. I had to sign something because they wanted to take him to the hospital. It would have no warning signs, he would be perfectly fine, then all of a sudden, he would be seizing. He wasn't sick before he started seizing; while he was having a seizure, we could feel his head getting hot. It happened several times, but even though we knew exactly what to do for them, it never got any easier. I hated seeing my little man lie there, not being able to help him. We would talk to him to let him know we were there, and little by little, he would start to move. I don't even think he remembered what happened.

Andrew taught himself how to read with Leap Frog videos. The first time I noticed he could read was at a friend's house. He read something on the TV, and I was shocked. He sounded it out. He was getting really good at reading. We could tell in other areas he was slower than the average child. He got tested in school for learning disabilities. He was diagnosed with ADHD and other learning disabilities. The doctor said he had fetal alcohol syndrome. I was a little mad at God for giving us a child who needed special care and needs. I really fell short at being a mother. I didn't have the patience I thought a mother should have for a child with special needs. I didn't have patience, period. I didn't think I could handle this again. Why would God do this to us again? Was it because we didn't do it right the first time? Was he giving us another chance? I have to believe there was a reason for it. I was very upset and had to start praying very hard.

I was still homeschooling Danielle, but things between her and some of the other homeschoolers got a little hairy. Friendships were breaking up. She needed to get into a school. We knew of another community that had their own private Catholic school, and we decided to send her there. It wasn't very close to where we lived, and I had to drive her there every day. It took an hour to get there. Then I got the hang of it and knew the right time to leave and made it there in forty-five minutes. It was a great school with many holy teachers. I think that school saved her from the misery she was going through with some of the homeschoolers. The school was a God-sent. I learned I had done a lot of things wrong, but the one thing I did right was putting all my kids in the Blessed Mother's hands. She would take care of the things I wasn't good at, and she did. I love Mama Mary. She has never let me down. She has been a great mother to me and my kids, especially Danielle.

Chapter Twenty

A faithful friend is a sturdy shelter; he who finds one finds a treasure. A faithful friend is beyond price, no sum can balance his worth. (Sirach 6:14–15)

I met my best friend Sarah through church. Her daughter Jaclyn became best friends with my daughter Danielle. The first time we got the girls together was on the Fourth of July. We went to the beach to see the fireworks. Jaclyn fell in love with Andrew, would love to come over and play with him. Ever since that Fourth of July, they became best friends.

Sarah was a convert like me. We also had a lot in common. Her husband's name was James, and she had a son named James who became friends with my son James. Her middle name is Danya. She grew up a lot like me, with a lot of the same situations. She was short like me, with curly black hair. I loved the way she gives hugs, like she hasn't seen me in years, she holds on so tight and long. We would go to daily Mass together. Now I hardly go during the week, but she still makes it to Mass every day. She loves God and has a devotion to St. Therese and Our Lady of Guadalupe. She is a prayer warrior.

I could tell Sarah anything. We became like sisters. I called her my family. Also Dena, whom I had lost touch with for a while, moved to New Jersey. We became close again. She is my best friend too. She has three sons, who all wound up in the navy (two are out now, one still in). I knew them since they were babies. I'm very proud to know them. Dena is a great mother; she always put her boys first. She is a great friend. I could tell her anything. Plus she knew me when I was younger and knew all my struggles. I thought of her as a sister too. I love my two best friends. I couldn't have gone through some of the things I did without them. I came to love Sarah's daughter Jaclyn as my own daughter and Dena's sons like my nephews. They became family to me. I love them and their families very much.

We were still going to healing Masses and retreats. We were baptized in the Holy Spirit. I would ask people to pray over me. I wanted to be healed from the memories of the past, especially the memory of my uncle Hank. I still had trouble making love to my husband. Thank God, I had an understanding man. James had his faults, but he was a great husband and father. He would do anything and everything for us. James was also very romantic. He would bring me flowers for no reason. We started going once a week on date night. We had learned date night was very important for a couple, when we went on a marriage retreat. He always remembered the things I liked. One memory in particular, he remembered I liked to watch Jerry Lewis movies when I was young and how much they made me laugh. One Christmas, he got me the whole set of Jerry Lewis movies. I was so touched that he remembered that. He would always say he loved me and I was the most beautiful girl he knew, even though I didn't think so.

I was never happy with the way I looked. My nose was too big, and I had gained weight. I was too short, and my thighs were too big. I was very hard on myself. I struggled with depression, which didn't help matters any. I had very low self-esteem. I wasn't feeling good and found out I had low blood sugar and had to change the way I was eating. I would get so dizzy at times, I thought I would faint and had to eat something to make me feel better. It wasn't easy, but I had to change my diet. After a few weeks, I started to feel a lot better. Slowly, I was recovering, and I lost some weight too. That made me happy.

We went into a business with friends of ours, Margaret and Vinny. We bought a Christian bookstore. It was already established; we knew the owners. A few years later, we bought a building with four families and put the bookstore in there and rented out three stores. We are more of a silent partner in the bookstore. The other couple runs it, and they are doing a great job. Margaret had a gift for arranging things. She does a beautiful job in decorating the store. Vinny is just so funny. He takes care of the sales and ordering of merchandise, but he does so much more; he really takes great care of the costumers. They all love him. They are wonderful people.

I wanted to adopt again, this time from China. I wanted a little girl. The paperwork was much harder for China than South Korea. A lot more stuff had to be done to adopt from China. We almost stopped the adoption because it was taking so long and we were getting older. We started the process right after Andrew was legally ours. I started a novena to St. Therese, asking her if we were going to get this child. I got an answer almost right away. While I was still doing my nine-day novena, I got an e-mail from one of my nieces; in the e-mail was a picture of a bunch of roses in all colors. That's how she answers prayers, with roses. Under the roses was a prayer to St. Therese. I was so excited, I got my answer! I told James about it, and we decided to wait longer for her. It felt like the call was never going to come. It took almost four years to finally get matched with a child.

We had moved again into another house. It was attached to another house (duplex), the inside was big, and the backyard was very big. We moved with another family next door. A few years later, that other family had to move. We got another friend to move in to that house. The Amato family. They were looking for something bigger. We are blessed to have them as neighbors. They are a wonderful family with two boys and two boys in heaven. I was blessed to have known her saints in heaven. That family was a beautiful testimony to God's love.

Chapter Twenty-One

Blessed are they who mourn, for they will be comforted. (Matthew 5:4)

While we were waiting, one day I had lots of pains in my stomach and sides. It got so bad, I asked James to take me to the hospital. While we were waiting for test results, the doctor came in and told us I was pregnant. We looked at each other in shock. I couldn't get pregnant, my tubes were clogged. For a moment, we were very happy. They took me for a sonogram and couldn't find the baby. Then the doctor told us the baby was in my tubes. My heart dropped. I couldn't believe God would let me get pregnant and then take the baby from me. I was devastated. In one day, I found out I was pregnant; the same day, I couldn't keep the baby.

I had to take a medication to dissolve my baby. I was going once a week for bloodwork to make sure the baby was gone. That was the hardest thing to do. Later, I realized God did give me a gift. I wanted so bad to become pregnant, and he allowed it. And I had another baby in heaven. I would see both of them one day. The day I found out I was pregnant was December 13, the feast day of St. Lucy, so that is what I named her. I had never named the baby I aborted, so I gave her the name Lucy. I had to go through Christmas with this pain of losing my baby. It was a rough time, but I put my best face on for the kids. I wanted them to have a great Christmas and to be excited about adopting another baby, which they were.

Two weeks later, on December 30, we got the call from the adoption agency; they had found us a baby. I was happy but had mixed feelings about it. I had just lost a baby and didn't feel like celebrating. I felt like if I was happy, I was betraying the baby I lost.

I was still sad and wanted to stay that way. But once we got her picture, I knew she was our daughter. We named her Therese because of the novena to St. Therese. We found out we were going to China in late February. We asked our daughter Danielle if she wanted to come with us. We would be in China for Danielle's and James's birthday. Danielle was very excited. James was too, but he was afraid to get on the plane. James promised me he would shave his hair before we left. And he kept his word. I shaved his head. We started to make travel plans to China.

We packed our bags and left for China with joy and excitement. James hated to fly, and the flight was twenty-four hours. He was not happy about that. It was a long flight, and I didn't sleep a bit. I could never sleep on planes; they are too uncomfortable. We made it to China and had to spend three days in Beijing doing paperwork. They did take us on a tour to the Forbidden City. We liked it, took lots of pictures. Then we went off on our own to see the Great Wall of China. It was funny because all the people looked at us like we were celebrities; there were two people who wanted to take their picture with us. We had a great time walking around the market, looking at all the weird things they ate. Danielle and James said they were going to try a scorpion on a stick, but they chickened out.

After our three days were up in Beijing, we had to fly to Guangzhou. That was the province Therese was from. And all the other stuff we had to do was in Guangzhou. We went to the office where you first meet your child. We waited a while for the buses to come with all the children that were being adopted. They brought them in a room and called us one by one. Everyone was getting their babies; it felt like we were waiting a long time. Finally it was our turn, and we went to get her. She looked scared and didn't hear a peep out of her. We took turns holding her. She bonded first with James. She liked to touch his face. It was great feeling her in my arms. James and I had tears in our eyes. We had to stay there for a while to talk to the caregivers. Therese started to cry hysteric. I felt so bad because we were strangers to her. She was scared of us.

That day we got to take her back with us to the hotel; from that moment on, she would always be with us. After a few days, she started to warm up to us, started smiling and laughing. She was adorable! She wasn't walking yet, and she was almost two years old. She also couldn't pick up Cheerios with her fingers. That worried me a little. She only ate chicken congee and rice.

While in China, James and I got sick. I was in bed for a couple of days. James and Danielle took Therese everywhere they needed to go. At this point, I couldn't wait to go home. While James was sick, I took Danielle and Therese out to dinner to celebrate Danielle's birthday. We were there for more than two weeks. We did some shopping for Therese, buying her a present for her birthdays until she was eighteen. We got her a pearl necklace and bracelet, and Danielle and I got one too.

We had to spend our last night in Hong Kong. Hong Kong looked so lit up; we arrived there at night. The hotel was so nice there. I had wished we could have stayed there longer. The next day, we had to fly home from there. We flew back, and I realized I left my camera in the hotel. I was so upset. It was a good thing Danielle had her own camera; she took tons of pictures. That would have stunk so much if I didn't have any pictures of China.

She still wasn't walking. When we got home, we took her to a neurologist, and they just said it was from being in a crib a lot in China. When she did start to walk, she would walk on her toes and fell down all the time. She was delayed in talking too. We got her early intervention. They worked with her speech and taught her sign language and physical therapy. The sign language helped a lot; she could tell us what she wanted.

Finally, we found the right doctor for her. They took a head scan and found out she had periventricular leukomalacia (PVL for short). PVL is something like a baby stoke; it happens when a baby is premature. It was a mild case, and from that, it gave her cerebral palsy in her leg. When she started school, she would get physical therapy, occupational therapy, and speech twice a week.

We also got a doctor for her legs. He recommended putting casts on her legs along with Botox shots to stretch her legs; she didn't have good mobility in her ankles. That is why she walked on her toes and fell a lot. We had to go get new casts every week to stretch her more. We did that for four to five months, and then they gave her braces for her legs at night. We kept her in pre-kindergarten for three years. It was only allowed to be two years, but I convinced them to keep her another year. It was good for her. Her speech was getting better, and she was walking better too.

Chapter Twenty-Two

My cousin Charlene got married. She seemed very happy, and I was very happy for her. She was a pediatrician working in the emergency room at the hospital. She was married for two years when she gave us the great news she was pregnant. I was so excited! She had a baby girl that looked just like her. She is adorable! She was very happy. I couldn't wait to meet her and hold her. Then about two and a half years later, she had a boy; he looked like his daddy. He is adorable too! I love those kids! They are very smart like their mommy. They lived in Boston. We visit them sometimes and stay over, or they come visit us. I love being with them. It's too bad they live so far away. I would like the kids to be able to see more of each other. I think we connect so well because we were both raised by sick mothers and no fathers. She took a bad situation and turned it to good. I'm very proud of her. She worked very hard to get where she is now. She is still working, but I think she cut down her hours. She spends quality time with her children. She is teaching them good morals, and she is always reading with them. She is a very strong person. I admire her a lot.

On March 17, we were in Aruba, we were having a great vacation. It was only the second day, but we got in so much stuff. We walked from one part of the island to another. We got in beach time and shopping time. One night on the beach, we were relaxing on a very comfy couch; there was a bar and I was sipping on a tropical drink. There was a nice cool breeze. We were enjoying just sitting on a comfy couch, listening to the waves crashing on the shore. It was very romantic. We were the only ones there, and the bartender said it was last call.

Then my cell phone started ringing, and I saw it was my cousin Charlene. All of a sudden, my heart dropped. Why would she be calling me while I was on vacation? It must be about my grand-mother. She was in the hospital. I said hello, and Charlene told me Grandma had passed away today. I was so upset, I had to give James the phone, and I started to cry. I couldn't talk. James finished talking to Charlene and sat next to me and just held me. She had just gotten sick not too long ago, and the doctors said she had cancer. She was turning yellow, so she went into the hospital for a procedure and it didn't go well, but she was herself and was going to go home soon. We decided not to tell her about the cancer, at least not yet.

She was talking to Liza and Charlene that day in the hospi-tal. She sounded good, Charlene said. She was talking about going home maybe tomorrow. Then they left, and an hour later, the hospi-tal called with the news. It went so fast. I thought my grandmother would never die. This sounds ridiculous because everybody has to die sometime. She was in her nineties. But I really didn't think of her ever dying. James and I had to get home; we called the airport and got a flight out the next day. I couldn't believe she was gone.

I was afraid to tell my mother. I didn't know how she would react. When I told my mom, she cried. She kept on saying how much she missed her mom. A couple of weeks before this, we went to visit her, and she looked so yellow and frail. I was glad Charlene suggested it because we all got to spend some time with her. I felt really bad for my aunt Liza because Grandma started living with her when Liza got her second divorce. She lived with her for a long time.

I was upset that I didn't see her at the hospital before she passed, but it was a blessing that it went so fast. My grandma had pancreatic cancer, and it already spread. She went peacefully in her sleep. She didn't have to go through all the pain that comes with cancer. When I first found out she was sick, I had prayed that she wouldn't have to go through pain. She was ninety-two years old.

We buried her in a Jewish cemetery that she already had a plot picked out for herself. It was a very sad day, saying good-bye to my grandmother. Never again would I get her calls saying, "Did you forget you had a grandmother!" In the Jewish religion, they wrap the body in white cloth and put them in a plain pine coffin. It's all done in one day, funeral and burial. They don't expose the body like at a

Christian wake. So right before they were going to bury her, we asked them if we could see her. They opened the coffin for us, and each of us got to touch her and say good-bye.

My grandmother was a very nervous person. She worried about everything and everybody. One day, my aunt Liza went on a trip. We went to visit her and keep her company. We took her out to dinner, and all she could think of was, "Why isn't Liza calling me? She should have gotten off the plane by now." Liza was late calling her, and my grandma was freaking out, almost in tears. She thought the plane went down or something else was wrong. She kept on calling my aunt's phone. I told her the flight was probably delayed. She could not relax. She couldn't eat her food; we had to leave the diner. While we were in the car, Liza called. Thank God! She was driving me crazy.

When I was first married, my grandma would call me every day, asking me if I left the burners on the stove. She also would tell me to make sure my door was locked and don't stand too close to the edge of the platform at the train station. She also believed her dreams were telling her something. If someone died in her dreams, that meant someone was going to die. Or if you dreamt about all your teeth falling out, that also meant someone was going to die. My grandma was very superstitious, no going under a ladder or opening an umbrella in the house. If the kids were lying on the floor, you couldn't walk over them, and if you did, you had to walk back over them or else they wouldn't grow. I would tell her that none of that stuff was true. I also told her those things are not of God. I would pray for her a lot. Every time she would tell me a dream and what it meant, I would ask her, "Did God make you a prophet?" She would laugh and continue to ask me what I thought it meant. I would tell her it's just a dream, unless you are a prophet.

She was a cute little grandma. I was going to miss all the stuff that drove me crazy. My aunt Liza was going through her stuff, and she found a letter she wrote to a saint, asking for prayer for all of her family. She mentioned all of us individually. She did listen to me when I talked about Jesus and the saints. I asked Liza to make a copy of it for me. I brought her a Bible, and I think she did read some of it. What I wouldn't do to walk arm in arm again and to feel her soft mushy skin.

Chapter Twenty-Three

It is the Lord who marches before you; He will be with you and will never fail you or forsake you. So do not fear or be dismayed. (Deuteronomy 31:8)

I was starting to feel sorry for myself yet again. Everything seemed to be getting harder for me. The kids were hard to handle. I was tired all the time, depressed, started to believe I had no worth. I had done nothing in my life worth mentioning. I would have liked to have a career. Something I was passionate about. There was nothing besides my children that I was proud of. I didn't read well, and that stopped me from trying things. I was a frightened little girl; I feared everything. I was so tired of being a failure. Everybody thought I had everything together, but I felt like I was living a lie.

I started having panic attacks. A few times I went to the hospital because I thought I was dying. I had a panic attack one day during a daily Mass. I left the church and went to my car. I felt very weird, and it scared me. I called up my best friend Sarah, but she wasn't home. Sarah's husband answered the phone. He could tell something was wrong. I told him I wasn't feeling well and that I couldn't drive. He came right away to pick me up. I told him I wanted to go to the hospital, and he drove me there. I wound up leaving because I knew it was a panic attack, and I was starting to feel better.

I always diagnosed myself. I would research all my symptoms online. I diagnosed my milk allergy, my gluten sensitivity. My life felt like it was falling apart. Another panic attack, I had was in bed going to sleep. I had to wake James up. It was so bad my whole body shook, and I thought I was going to die. My doctor gave me some Xanax, but I didn't want to take it. Taking new meds made me have anxiety.

But that night was bad, James told me to take it, so I took a half of one. It worked and got me to sleep. I had to go on another anxiety pill every day. It was a small dose, but it did the trick. Those attacks were so frightening. It was the worse feeling in the world.

My daughter Danielle went to college for one year in Pennsylvania and then took a year off to do service work in Belgium. I was so proud of her. She got to see a lot of places in Europe. While I was going through my breakdown, I wrote a very serious letter to James on how I was feeling. I was never good at talking things out. I told him I felt like getting on a plane and leaving everything behind. That meant him and the kids. That's how distraught I was. I would cry all the time. So James told me to go visit Danielle in Belgium. I got on a plane and flew to Belgium. I was so happy to see Danielle! She took me on tours, saw beautiful churches, and even spent a couple of days in Paris. It was a wonderful trip. It gave me some time to forget all my troubles. I was able to just be. No worries. I met Danielle's roommates and the community that was there. Everybody I met was so nice. I got to see the Eiffel Tower and the Louvre. I was so excited to see the *Mona Lisa*. I lost Danielle in the Louvre, the place was so big, but we found each other. One night at the Eiffel Tower, there was a bomb scare. There were police getting everyone away from the Tower. We started to walk back to our hotel. Danielle was very scared. For some reason, I didn't think it was real, and it wasn't. We got to do a lot of things, but I was very tired. When it was time to go home, I didn't want to leave Danielle.

James stayed home and took care of the kids. He is a great husband and father. A few things that bothered me about him, I wrote in the letter. When I got home, he worked very hard to fix those things. James was starting to act a little different. I liked it. And I worked hard on myself to be a better wife and mother. It wasn't always easy, but I kept on working through it. He would take care of the kids on the weekends to give me a break. He is a hands-on dad and loves to spend time with his family.

I started to love the image of Our Lady of Guadalupe. I prayed for her to intercede for us. I started to pray more for everything. One of my biggest prayers was answered. God healed me! I was able to make love to James without thinking of my uncle. It was a true miracle! We made love like it was the first time, every time. We felt like teenagers. It was the greatest feeling. I wanted to shout it out on the rooftops. I was healed! I was even able to share this miracle with some young couples that were having some of the same troubles. There have been many miracles I have seen in my lifetime, but this one was the most important one for me. Not only was I able to make love to my husband, I also started to communicate much better with James. I saw him in a different way. And whenever we got into an argument, it wouldn't last long. We got along really well. It was so great!

There were a few miracles my daughter Danielle had. I prayed to our Blessed Mother, and she would take care of her. I asked Mother Mary to show Danielle her son and she did. One miracle was what I called the miracle of the warts. Danielle used to pick the skin off her fingers. She had a wart on one of her fingers that started to spread to all her fingers until she had about thirty warts in all. I took her to a dermatologist, and she started to treat her one finger each time. After her third treatment, I went to a healing Mass and prayed for Danielle, and it wasn't to heal her warts; it was just she had been going through a lot at the time. I also prayed to Mother Mary. The next day, Danielle woke up and came to me. She looked a little confused. She told me she had no more warts on her hands and showed me her hands. I started to yell out, "You had a miracle!" She thought I was crazy. I wanted to see the doctor's reaction, so I took her to the next appointment. I showed the doctor her fingers and told her it was a miracle. I mentioned I had gone to a healing Mass. On the next healing Mass, I saw her and some coworkers at that Mass. What a great witness to the healing power of God. The thing is that we humans tend to forget the miracles we see. Just like Peter denying he knew Jesus three times. Or the devil makes us think it was just a coincidence.

Chapter Twenty-Four

Yet the Lord is waiting to show you favor, and he rises to pity you; For the Lord is a God of justice: blessed are all who wait for Him! (Isaiah 30:18)

As each has received a gift, use it to serve one another, as good stewards of God's varied grace: (1 Peter 4:10)

James and I started to minister to a few young couples who had just gotten married. They would ask us about our marriage and how we made it work for so long. We just told them about all our experiences, good and bad, and that seemed to help them. And that we couldn't do it without God. Things were looking up, and I was very happy. We still had to work on our marriage. We worked very hard to keep our marriage fresh and new. We had to put us before the kids. The order of God: God comes first of course, spouses, kids, and then everything else. We learned how to listen to each other and be kind to each other even if we didn't feel like it at that moment. I learned to let God control things; it turned out better that way. When I tried to control things, I always messed it up. Prayer became very important. I would have been crushed by some of my circumstances if I didn't have God. Every morning before I and the kids wake up, James prays over all of us before he leaves for work. He does a rosary in his car to work. He keeps his family spiritually safe. I know he would lay down his life for me and his children. I also couldn't have made it through some of my rough times without his prayers. A spouse's prayers are powerful. Hoping his prayers get me into heaven.

My mother still lived in an assisted living in Coney Island, the worst neighborhood. She got mugged walking to the store, and the workers would steal all the stuff we would buy her. They also stole money from her. We got a call one day that my mom fell and was in Coney Island Hospital. We went to visit her; her shoulder was broken. We decided to take her to our house to recover.

I didn't like the place where my mom was living, so I decided to keep her with us. I didn't want to see her living in a place like that all her life. She deserved better. She lived with us for maybe two years before we found an assisted living place not too far from us. The place was like a palace compared to the place in Brooklyn. It was clean, and it didn't smell. They had nice furniture in the common areas. There was a nice dining area.

We took her on a couple of vacations. We took her to Disney World with another family, and she sat in a wheelchair. We pushed her everywhere. She had fun. She had never been anyplace but NYC. We also took her to a hotel in Pennsylvania with friends of ours. She was happy. The doctors found a good medicine for her, and her voices were gone for a while. It was so nice to be able to take her places without her talking to herself. It was so great to be able to take her places and also talk to her without all those demons in her head. This was the first time I got to enjoy her. I wasn't embarrassed anymore. It was like I have somewhat of a real mother.

James and my mom became very good friends. They would make each other crack up with laughter. He would pick her up, and on the way to my house, they would listen and sing to Doo-Wop music. My mother loved the oldies. (I grew up on Doo-Wop, heard it in my house so much, I knew all the words to all the songs.) James took better care of my mother than I did.

On Christmas and her birthday, we would give her presents, and she would love everything. She appreciated everything we did for her, and everything we got her. It was like she was getting gold but meanwhile it could be a cheap little bracelet that Andrew or Therese got her from school. She was like a kid opening up presents and loving everything she got.

I'm so glad we brought her to New Jersey. She was happy to be near her family. It gave her a lot of pleasure to be able to see us so often. She told everybody where she lived about all of us, with such joy on her face. She would introduce James as her handsome son-in-law. She loved all of James's family. She would come to all events with us. But toward the end, her medicine stopped working. She wasn't as bad as she used to be, and you could still have a conversation with her, but the demons came back and she would talk to them and curse sometimes. I had to stop taking her to things. We would celebrate holidays on different days with her.

Then Mom got sick, and in the hospital, they found out she had pancreatic cancer. We took her to a doctor, and they said it was too bad to treat. We didn't tell her; she would have been scared. She was put in a nursing home where she passed away. My mother also went fast, with very little pain. I was just so happy that I was with her when she passed from this life to her eternal life with Jesus. I never want to forget her; she was the most loving person I know.

Chapter Twenty-Five

For I know well the plans I have in mind for you, says the Lord, plans for your welfare, not for woe! Plans to give you a future full of hope. (Jeremiah 29:11)

My daughter Danielle finished college with honors. I was so proud of her. She was the first one in our family to go to college. She was a teacher! Danielle fell in love with a young man and moved to Minnesota to be close to him. She was there a little over a year. Things wound up not working out between them. She came back home. I was happy to have her home. I didn't like her so far away from me. She is upset her relationship had to come to an end. It will hurt for a while, but she is strong and will get through it. She has her best friend and us to help her through it.

I felt Danielle's pains and happiness. I used to tell her she was my heart. She had gone through a lot throughout her life. She was so smart and courageous. In my eyes, she was the bravest person I know. Danielle is a beautiful girl with the heart of gold. Her future husband will be very lucky to have her. Danielle deserves only the best. She is a child of God; her Father, the King will show his princess the way. Danielle is on another journey. I hope it takes her places that will change her life forever in a great way. I can't wait to see what God has in store for her.

She just got a new teaching job and will start very soon. She is great with children. She went out and bought a bunch of stuff for her new class and even painted the bathroom in her room with her dad. I know the kids in her new class will love her. I pray that this year is going to be a great year for her. She is also planning to move out with some friends. She misses being on her own and out of her parent's house, which I can't blame her. She doesn't have the privacy she used to have. It's hard being on your own for so long then having to go back home to mom and dad.

> Jesus looked at them and said, for human being
> it is impossible, but not for God. All things are
> possible with God. (Mark 10:27)

My son James Jr. is working in St. Mary's Church. He used to work for us in our religious bookstore, but he got bored of that. He had other jobs like being Chuck E. Cheese and being an exterminator, but working for the church and babysitting was his thing. He was happy. He is driving and working and doing very well for himself. I am very proud of the man he has become.

He was always a loving child and still is. He is a hugger, and he always tells me he loves me, at night before bed and saying good-bye on the phone. He is very respectful to all the people he knows and meets. When he walks into a room, he makes sure he shakes all the men's hands in the room and kisses the entire women hello. He is a very caring person. I just wished he would clean his room. He has some rough days; most of his cousins are married with kids. Even though James Jr. knows everybody, he doesn't have a friend that he can hang out with. I pray a lot for him. All he does is work and stay home, playing videogames or watching TV. He knows he is a little different than other men his age.

He went through a really dark place once, blaming God for him being the way he was. My husband, James, does a lot with him. They get season tickets to the Red Bulls games and go to hockey and basketball games too. James Jr. loves sports and has a great time with his father. I would be thrilled if Andrew turns out as good as James Jr. James Jr. has a pure heart.

> I am the Lord, the God of all mankind! Is any-
> thing impossible to me? (Jeremiah 32:27)

My son Andrew is a funny guy. He has the cutest smile and loves to laugh. He says the cutest things. He taught himself to read and reads very well, but he has a hard time comprehending what he is reading. He is doing well in school; he is in a Special Education class. He got great grades this year and was on the honor roll. He can also be very loving. He loves music and loves dancing. He doesn't have much rhythm, but it's so cute to watch him dance, and he has a ball doing so. Andrew takes piano, and he used to do karate but he quit. Sometimes it's hard to get him there, but once he is there, he likes it. We just signed him up for the children's choir at church. His piano teacher is in charge of that. He is and has been in the choir at school and loves it. I love to watch him sing. I'm so proud of him. And you could hear him; he is loud.

When I give him a reward for behaving, he hugs me and tells me, "I love you, Mommy." He is an angel at Mass. He follows all the readings and sings all the songs. He is getting taller and older looking. The baby face is going away. He is a very handsome young man. It's such a pleasure to be around Andrew when he is good. But when he is having one of his episodes, I want to pull the hair out of my head, and I don't want to be around him. I feel terrible that I feel this way. Then I start to think of what is going on in his head. He can't control himself. He was diagnosed with Asperger's; he has a rough time socializing.

This year, he is in sixth grade and made his very first friend. His friend came over for a play date. They started to Facetime and text each other. His friend has his own phone, but Andrew has to use mine. He has trouble getting off his videogames. He screams and cries a lot; it's part of his disability. We took away his iPod, and he is doing better but now he is hooked on Power Rangers. That is all he wants to do. Now it is hard to get him away from the TV.

Sometimes I think I'm too hard on him and expect too much. I have a hard time dealing with him. He doesn't like to lose when he is playing a game; he will cry. And the older he gets, the more he is talking back to me. He will tell me to shut up and say that I'm stupid. And *no* is his favorite word. He doesn't realize if he doesn't stop his bad behavior, he will get into trouble.

The hormones are kicking in too. He is getting worse and very hard for James and me to handle. He is getting bigger and stronger, I'm afraid of him hurting himself or others. He has said he will hit his sister and the dog. We need help for him to learn how to control his emotions. We need help to know how to better deal with him. We just want peace in the house.

He can't express his feelings the right way. He doesn't want to be like this. But we are now seeing a behavioral specialist. It is helping him to learn how to control his emotions and help us to know how to treat him when he acts out. We need tools to take care of him. He is growing up so quickly. James is reading a book on autism, and we are starting to understand him more and treat him differently. I am also trying to let go of him a little and stop treating him like a baby. I was doing too many things for him. He needs to learn how to be independent. I think I'll show Andrew how to do the laundry.

But with the help of God and that book, we are learning so much and being more patient with him. We are starting to see the fruits of our labor. He is talking more to other people and playing with more than just his sister. The school he goes to is wonderful and is teaching him how to be with others and be more independent. We are seeing some light at the end of the tunnel. It is still going to be a struggle at times. He is a wonderful boy that has some problems but has a family who loves him very much. And we will do anything to help him. Now he is into game shows. He is almost as tall as I am now. By next year, he will be taller than little old me. He is going into seventh grade. I can't believe it!

Therese is quite a character. She can have a conversation with you that will blow your mind. I think she is brilliant. She knows so much stuff. She will ask questions all day long. She wants to know about everything. And what an imagination she has. Therese's toys are my recycling bin. She uses cardboard, paper, and plastic bottles to invent things. She loves tape! She doesn't play with regular toys and hates dolls; she'd rather use her imagination. She is good at soccer, and she did karate for almost two years before she quit that. I thought she was good at karate, but she said there was too much exercise. She makes up her own jokes; sometimes they make no sense at all, but she is funny. She uses some words the wrong way, which is cute. She has a great mind, and I have no doubt she will do big things when she gets older.

Therese was not a good reader at first. She was getting lazy and didn't even want to try. We had to put her in a special reading class, and she was doing a lot better. Besides that, she is very good in school. She remembers everything she learns. She would come home from school and teach me things. She is good in science and social studies.

Therese is not shy at all; she will talk to anybody. She can talk to an adult, and they are usually amazed at what she knows and how well she can keep up with the conversation. She won't sing or dance in front of anybody but has no problem talking. She gets along with everyone she meets. She is always happy except when she loses. She likes to win and is a sore loser; she could win ten games in a row and then lose one, then that's it for her; she gets angry and then gives up. She is definitely a perfectionist.

One day when she was in school, I got a call from the nurse telling me she was hysterical. I rushed over there, and she was in the nurse's office with the nurse on one side of her holding her hand and the principal on the other side of her holding her hand, both talking to her and trying to calm her down. Her hands were in a fist, and they were locked in that position. The nurse said she tightened her body. The teacher came to talk to me and told me this happened because she made a mistake on her paper and tried to erase it, but the paper got a small hole in it. She flipped out because she didn't finish her work and wanted to go to recess. The teacher tried to tell her it wasn't a big deal and she could get a new paper, but by then, she couldn't control herself. I tried to talk to her while the nurse and principal rubbed her hands so they would open. I got scared; I started to cry but with my head turned so she wouldn't see me. I said what is wrong with her hands? Then I saw her old preschool teacher walk past the door. Therese had her for three years, and she loved her. I told someone to get her, and she came in and talked to Therese. She told her there was nobody in her classroom, she asked Therese if she wanted to go with her and play with some toys. Therese said yes, and her hands opened a little. She went to her classroom, and then she was fine. I was able to leave her in school the rest of the day.

This happened again at home once. She also has separation anxiety. She won't sleep over at her cousin's house. She tried two times, and I had to pick her up. If I leave her at home with a babysitter, she is fine. I never tried leaving her somewhere with her brother. Maybe that would make a difference. It upsets her when she gets yelled at, but she really is very good and hardly gets yelled at.

She does this thing we call nip nip. She was doing it when we first met her. She nips on her arm and my arm or face. She places her lips on us and moving them like she is sucking on something; it is her comforter. She can't stop doing it. Just like Danielle has always twirled her hair even as a baby and still does. She was left in her crib alone a lot in China, so she had to find a way to comfort herself.

She is definitely one of a kind. She loves to give hugs, and she gives long ones. She doesn't like to be kissed though. She has touched the lives of some in a special way. You can't know her and not love her. She has a good heart and cares about people. She told me one day that she was going to China when she gets older and change the rules there about having one kid. I really believe she will do amazing things, and maybe she can change the world. Maybe she will be the first woman president. Therese is a leader, not a follower, which I love about her. She doesn't care what people think about her. She does what makes her happy. The friends she has picked in school are wonderful girls. She always tries to do the right thing.

Chapter Twenty-Six

Boast not of tomorrow, for you know not what
any day may bring forth. (Proverbs 27:1)

One day we went to an aquarium with good friends of ours. It wasn't close; it took an hour to get there. It was a very hot day. We had our niece with us. We had a nice time, but James said he wasn't feeling well. I saw him holding his chest. On the way home, James started to feel worse. We stopped at a rest stop for Advil, and he sat outside on the back bumper of the van for a while. He asked me to drive. While I was driving, I looked over at him, and he was holding his chest and he sounded like he was in pain. He told me to pull over on the parkway because he couldn't breathe. He told me that I was a good wife, and that freaked me out. I got scared.

I pulled over in the middle of a ramp. Cars were passing us on both sides. He got out of the van and went to the back of the van. He told me to stay in the car, and he would call the friends that we were with. I looked back and didn't see him, so I got out of the van and walked around the van. He was on the ground. He was finding it hard to breathe. I told him I was going to call an ambulance, but he said he wanted to go home. A very nice couple saw him on the ground as they were driving on the parkway and stopped to see if we needed help. James still didn't want to call an ambulance, but the couple did. The man gave James a pillow for under his head. They stayed with us until the ambulance came. James still refused to go to the hospital. He told them if he still felt like this when we got home, he would then go to the hospital near us.

So we drove home, dropped off the kids, and I had to convince him to go. We went to the hospital near us and told them his symptoms. They did some tests on James, and a doctor came in and told him he had a pulmonary embolism. He said, "Okay, can I go home now?" He didn't believe the doctor; he said he would go to his doctor. A nurse came in and told James, "You don't understand, you can die if you go home and do nothing. You must stay in the hospital!" She continued to explained things to him, and then he started to believe how serious this really was. I was so scared, and he was too. We looked at each other, and I wanted to cry. James looked scared. James was in the hospital for a few days; they treated him and told him to see a hematologist. That doctor put him on blood thinners.

I could have lost him that day if he didn't go to the hospital! That was so scary. He is doing well now and is off the blood thinners and is on a baby aspirin. Thank God he went to the hospital when he did. That was a wakeup call. We are getting older and really need to take good care of ourselves and make sure we go get all our annual checkups. I think that day made us think more about our age and our mortality. We are in the next generation where now we know friends who have passed away. It makes you really think about death and how long we have left on this earth. Have we lived up to our potential? Have we helped enough people along the way? I know I need to do more before I leave this earth.

Chapter Twenty-Seven

I have told you this so that you might have peace in me. In the world you will have trouble, but take courage, I have conquered the world. (John 16:33)

God is our refuge and our strength, an ever-present help in distress. Thus we do not fear, though earth be shaken and mountains quake to the depths of the sea. (Psalm 46:1–3)

Then I started getting tired all the time, my joints were hurting me, and my memory was getting bad. I always had a bad memory, but it was ridiculous the stuff I wasn't remembering. My head felt like it was in a fog. I would forget simple words and couldn't think. My nephew had found out he had Lyme, and he told me his symptoms. I had a lot of the same stuff. I went to the Lyme specialist that he went to, and they took some bloodwork, and the doctor told me I had Lyme disease. They started me on antibiotics, lots of them. The doctor said it would get worse before it gets better; she was right.

There were many days I couldn't get out of bed. And I got tired just walking up my stairs to my bedroom. This was very hard when you have two kids to take care of. How am I supposed to get my kids ready for school when I can't get out of bed? Sometimes my hands would shake so bad and I felt so nervous that I couldn't think straight. I was so confused, it scared me. It felt like my body was betraying me. I couldn't handle even little things. Everything made me feel overwhelmed and anxious. Sometimes I felt like I wasn't in my body. I cried all the time. It was becoming too much for me. I wasn't cleaning the house, and I like a clean house. Most days I couldn't cook for my family. I would have panic attacks. At night, my legs would get tingly and feel very weird. The antibiotic and the Lyme in my body were fighting each other; there was a war inside me. I was already on a no-dairy, no-gluten, and no-sugar diet. But the doctor said all grains would give me inflammation and make my joints hurt more.

I had to go on a strict diet. I only eat meat and vegetables, nothing high carb. I got an overabundance of candida in my body, had to go on an even stricter diet. This was killing me. I lost a lot of weight, went down to ninety-seven pounds, but wasn't exercising and losing all my muscles. I was weak and flabby. I felt so frail, like my body could break at any time. I wanted so much to be able to eat. I couldn't enjoy my food. After a few months on medicine for the candida and not eating anything, it got better. I started to eat a little more. Some of my Lyme symptoms got a little better. Still couldn't eat a lot of stuff, but it was better than the candida diet. I started to drink my Starbucks frappes again. I needed some enjoyment. When I tried to cheat on my diet, I felt it the next day. My body would hurt, and I would have a bad headache. When I cheat, I usually cheat bad. I'm a carb and sugar addict. Once I started, it took a while to get back to my diet. I'm feeling much better now, still have some ups and downs. I like my Lyme doctor; he gives me antibiotics but still believes in natural remedies. I found out I had a thyroid problem; my doctor put me on medicine for that. I was struggling with my diet, not being able to eat the things I liked.

I was struggling with a lot of things. I was struggling with my kids. They were getting harder to handle, especially with me being sick. Any little thing felt like chaos. James would help around the house and with the kids. I couldn't help but think I was a burden sometimes. I felt like some people didn't believe I had Lyme. Lyme started to get recognized more because some celebrities had it and they spoke up about it in the media.

Now I was in my fifties and in menopause. I started having intimacy problems with James. I got a little mad at God. I was finally healed of my sexual problems and now I'm in menopause! Are you kidding me! Why would God keep doing this to me? Didn't I suffer enough? Didn't sound like a God I wanted to know. What happened to the God that said, "Ask and it will be given to you; seek and you will find; knock and the door will be opened it you" (Matthew 7:7)? That was the God I wanted, to give me everything I asked for. I started to doubt God's existence. Well, I wanted to doubt. I knew he was there. I just decided to ignore him. I didn't even want to go to church anymore, but I did it for James and the kids. I felt bad for my husband. He had to deal with all my problems. But he is such a good man. Sometimes I thought I didn't deserve him. He deserved someone who could love him better. I had so much baggage. I wish God would heal me so I could be a better wife and mother. My family deserved a heathy wife and mother. It took me a while, but things got better, and I knew I had to come back to God. And I did get what I asked for at times, not in my time but in God's time. And the things I didn't get, only God knows why. I'm sure he has a good reason. If I make it to heaven, I will be sure to ask him.

Things still are tough in my life. I'm having a battle with food (all the foods I can't have). I find myself crying at times. It's too much to bear. I have a love affair with food (but not in a good way), and it depresses me so much. One day, I ate five cupcakes like I was a junky. They were paleo, but they had sugar in them. Anything sweet gets me going. I sat on my bed, and when my husband came home, I put my head on his chest and cried, "I can't stop eating." He prayed over me. I'm trying to stay away from sweets, but it is very hard for me, especially when there is so little I can eat. I'm getting bored with the same old foods. I just can't eat a little bit of the things I can't have. Once it hits my mouth I am done for. That is when I can't stop eating it. I have many crosses to bear.

Andrew is getting more difficult. I used to pray to God to fix Andrew. But he isn't broken; I am. Now I pray to fix myself. I have to learn how to deal with him. He can't help himself. It seems like one thing after another. I'm not in control of anything, and that's hard for me. I'm a control freak. I'm the one who wants to fix everything and everyone. That's my problem; I think I could fix it when only God can. I would look for answers online for how to cure autism. I tried diet, homeopathic, vitamins—anything I could try, I tried.

I really thought I could cure Andrew. Some of that stuff did make things better. The gluten/dairy-free diet helped a lot. He seemed like a different person when he was glutened.

My kids are getting so big, and time is flying by so quickly. I needed to get myself out of the funk I was in. I needed to start living a fulfilled life. I have a great life and a great family, but I wasn't fulfilled. Some of it was because of all the health issues and the depression I went through. But I was still very down on myself, like I could have done more with my life. I wish I had a passion for something. There was something missing in my life. I needed to do something for myself. I know God will help me solve this problem, if I only trusted in him more. God needed to give me the answers I was looking for. I needed to be able to love myself more. I wanted to do something that was important to me. Maybe even help others in some way. I needed something to feel good about, needed something to call my own. I needed something that I could be proud of. It was time for me to come out of my comfort zone. Make a change and not be afraid.

Chapter Twenty-Eight

The mind of the intelligent gains knowledge, and the ear of the wise seeks knowledge.
(Proverbs 18:15)

In all circumstances hold faith as a shield, to quench all flaming arrows of the evil one.
(Ephesians 6:16)

I have a handful of friends that I love very much. I also have a few friends who have broken my heart for no apparent reason to me. It's been years, and I still can't get over it. I really miss them. I wish things could go back to the way they were before. I pray for them, especially when I find myself getting mad at them. I don't like to feel unwanted. I wish I could just move on. I feel like I put a lot of effort into my friendships, only to be let down (not all of course). I'm used to Brooklyn life, when I would be able to see my friends almost every day. I was friends with my neighbors and hung outside of our houses. Jersey is different; nobody hangs out in front of their houses. Nobody just stops by for coffee. We would just stop by without calling. I miss city life. I don't miss the old neighborhood just the way things were. At times it gets a bit lonely in New Jersey. I like being with my family, but I'm a people person and need friends around me.

My kids call my friend Sarah Aunt. She loves them as much as I do. I asked Sarah to be Therese's godmother. She had my cousin Charlene for her godmother, and James's brother Tim is her godfather. But Charlene left the Catholic Church, so I thought she needed a godmother who believed the same way I did. Sarah was thrilled that I asked her. Sarah is the best godmother ever. She takes Therese to the chapel and teaches her about God. Therese is always asking about the saints, and her favorite one is Saint Michael. She also likes Saint Joan of Arc, whom I love too. Sarah brought her a big chest, and Therese calls it her holy chest. Everything Sarah gives her, she puts in it. Therese wears her St. Therese medal and her crucifix (that her godfather and aunt got her) around her neck and won't take it off, except for soccer because it's not allowed. Therese doesn't like church because she has to be quiet. But she does like learning about the faith. Sarah takes Therese out for her birthday and Christmas every year so she could pick out her own presents. Therese loves to do that. Her uncle Tim and aunt Doreen started doing that as well. They also take her to the diner for motzoh ball soup, her favorite! She loves spending time with her godparents. I think it is very special. Both godparents are very special people.

I started a Bible study with my two best friends, Sarah and Dena. Sarah has a gift of understanding scripture and what it means for us today. Sarah is helping me understand God's love through the scriptures. Dena and I are learning a lot. I'm starting to get it. I'm doing more things to help myself out of my depression. Things like getting out of the clothes I slept in, taking a shower, and getting dressed. I'm going back to the gym, which is good for my body and mind. Get out of the house and take a walk with the dogs. The big one is make sure I make my bed. When my bed is made, I feel like cleaning the whole house, and when my house is clean, I'm happy. I did have to get a cleaning lady once a week. I'm just too tired to clean my whole house, and when I do, the next day I'm in bed all day.

I hear God speaking to me now, through other people or scripture. I'm the happiest I have ever been. I still have a rough time with the kids at times, my Lyme is much better but have flare-ups every so often, and I have osteoporosis, but I know I'll be okay. I love my life with James and my kids, I'm blessed beyond belief. I have two dogs I love, Max and Ruby. I have a house I love and everything in it. I have great friends. I'm making my dreams come true. We travel a lot. What else do I need? God has giving me more than I thought I would ever have. And I know he has much more for me. I can't wait to find out what it is! And being totally honest about my struggles will allow me to help others. There are couples that needed to hear my story; it helped with their marriages. Just like there are people I needed to hear that are helping me. We all have something to contribute. If everyone helped each other out, what a wonderful world this would be.

At the age of fifty, I got my first tattoo. It was a tribute to my mom and all my children, even the ones in heaven. I had it put on my back near my neck. This tattoo was sort of a healing. I realized how great my mother really was, and I never felt like I acknowledged my babies in heaven. I need this tattoo to prove to myself I could honor all my children and Mom. A year later, I got another tattoo. I was hooked. But my tattoos had to have meaning to me. My next one was an infinity sign with the words "I love you to the moon and back." That is what I tell my kids. I'm getting another one on my wrist of a heart with the date my mom died, and it says, "Until I see you again." That should be my last one, but you never know.

> Give thanks to the Lord who is good, whose love
> endures forever! (Psalm 107:1)

James was doing very well in his job. He went higher and higher in the company. He had a good relationship with the owners of the company, and he loves his job. He made very good money, and we were able to do a lot more stuff. We had a nice house; it wasn't a mansion, but we didn't want a mansion. It was big for us. We were able to have nice things, but we were also very prudent with our money. We went on lots of trips. We both loved traveling. I think my favorite place so far is Puerto Rico. It's beautiful there, the water is so blue, and the food is to die for. There are a lot more places I would love to see. We are going to knock them off our bucket list. I love an adventure and to see places with history, like ancient ruins, old churches, and caverns. I would love to see all the places Jesus went. My dream trip is to go to Fiji and stay in a hut on the water. We were also able to help others when they needed it. It was important to help family members or friends in need. We are thinking of buying a house in Florida and becoming snowbirds. God has been very generous with us. We are so blessed. I have to realize that every day and thank God for all he has given us.

Chapter Twenty-Nine

Say to those whose hearts are frightened: Be strong, fear not! Here is your God, he comes with vindication; with divine recompense he comes to save you. (Isaiah 35:4)

God helped me get over some of my fears. I was always afraid of guns. Once I saw a real gun at my friend's cousin's house, it was just sitting on the table. I didn't know what was going on in that house. I just knew I wanted to get out of there and started to panic. Not too long ago, James and I went to a shooting range. I used a .22 caliber gun, a little bitty gun. I learned how to load it and shoot it. I really like it. I got it in the middle of the target a few times. I would definitely go back. I don't want to be afraid of them, especially in these crazy times we are living in. The world is becoming a very dangerous place. I want to be able to keep my family safe. I hope I never have to use one. I don't know if I'll ever buy one. Not against buying one, but it would be a huge responsibility owning a gun.

Another fear of mine was getting lost in my car. But driving a school bus was a blessing. There was no GPS back then, and I had to use a map. I learned quickly how to use it and make all the stops before school started. Highway driving scared me too. I would get panic attacks. Those went away also. Having to drive two hours a day on the parkway to get my older daughter to school took care of that. I think by then, I had a GPS. I see God taking my fears away one by one. I had another fear of calling and talking to people I didn't know on the phone. That one came from Grandma; she always made my aunt Liza make calls about bills and appointments. I slowly overcame that fear. Now I do all the calling and text my kids' teachers a lot too. So many times in the Bible, it talks about not fearing anything.

> Peace I leave with you; my peace I give to. Not
> as the world gives do I give it to you. Do not let
> your hearts be troubled or afraid. (John 14:27)

I always threw myself into television, which was the way I coped with things. I went into fantasy land making the people on the screen my family. Television became everything to me. I watched things I shouldn't have and couldn't stop myself. I think it was taking me away from my family. I had to stop watching some of my shows. It wasn't as easy as I thought. I was a television junky. But watching those things didn't let the Holy Spirit work in me. I would try to talk myself into thinking the shows were okay to watch, that I could love Jesus and watch them. After all, I knew it wasn't real, and I was now a grown-up. The devil put that in my head. That evil angel knew all my weaknesses. I used to get mad at my grandma for putting television before me. Now I was doing the very same thing I hated. In Romans 7:15, it says, "What I do, I do not understand. For I do not do what I want, but I do want I hate." That is me. I'm deleting all my shows that keep my away from God and my family. I pray I could be strong enough and to rely on God more to keep me away. This might not sound like a big deal to some, but it is a very big deal for me. I see the way God is trying to show me this, but I chose to ignore it. I should know better than to ignore him.

Do I still get afraid? Of course, I do. I'm only human. But now I'm less afraid. Now I know I shouldn't be afraid because Jesus told me so. Life isn't going to be perfect for me or anybody, but if we know who to go to for peace, we will be okay. Trusting in God isn't always easy; it's very hard work. We have to pray and never stop praying. I have the Blessed Mother who helps me when I feel Jesus slipping away. And it really is me slipping away, not Jesus. He is always with me. I just have to keep reminding myself of that. Even when I'm not feeling him, he is there even more. If you look very close, you'll see him there, not in the flesh but in all that is wonderful about this earth. We see him in some

DAWN LARGE

of the people we meet. Jesus is in the love of a spouse and children because he is love. We just have to pay attention and look for him.

I understand that when things get tough, it's hard to see Jesus because we are focused on our own grief, not on him. I have done that many times, thought only about myself. I still will do that at times. I'm a sinner just like everyone else. I'm a work in progress and will never get there until, hopefully, I'm in heaven.

My Lyme is acting up again a little. My stomach is all messed up. I can't eat anything without getting sick. It's hard to deal with this illness at times. I've been on antibiotics for years now, and it can't be good for my stomach. I did wind up stopping the antibiotics without telling my doctor. I just couldn't take it any longer. I talked to a few friends that have Lyme too. They were taking natural stuff to help them with their Lyme. They told me they were taking Himalayan salt in water, vitamin C, and detox fiber. Plus they had to drink buckets of water. I tried it. I had a good feeling about it. I have prayed about my Lyme, and I think God brought me to this friend. I feel tired, but I'm making it through. I'm still going to the gym and walking the dog even though I'm tired. I refuse to let this destroy me. I'm going to get worse before I get better. The salt is killing the Lyme and the vitamin C and detox fiber flushes all the toxins out of my body. There will be a battle going on in my body and in my mind once again.

After three weeks of doing this, I decided to stop the saltwater. It was getting me nauseous and giving me anxiety. I felt like I was bloated all the time, and I felt like I was going to float away with all that water. I would rather get body pain than have anxiety. I don't like when my Lyme messes with my mind. Panic attacks are the worst! I feel like I'm dying! I still continue to drink lots of water, take the vitamin C, and the detox fiber.

I have started a new probiotic and cleanse that sounds great. I've seen testimonials from people who have Lyme and these products work. I am praying it does. I need some relief.

> I commanded you: Be firm and steadfast. Do not
> fear nor be dismayed, for the Lord, your God, is
> with you wherever you go. (Joshua 1:9)

114

Chapter Thirty

Finally, draw your strength from the Lord and from his mighty power. Put on the armor of God so that you may able to stand firm against the tactics of the devil. (Ephesians 6:10–11)

Filled with the Holy Spirit, Jesus returned from the Jordan and was led by the Spirit into the desert for forty days, to be tempted by the devil. (Luke 4:1–2)

I will not let the devil get me down. Every time I feel like feeling sorry for myself, I just stop it and call on the Holy Spirit. I also ask Mother Mary for help, and I ask my mom in heaven to pray for me. I have so many people in heaven that are praying for me. I just got to keep on praying and get closer to God. I can't do it without him. My marriage is good (not perfect) and lasted this long because of God. We have to put him first in our marriage. I know God put James and me together. We are soulmates. Yes, there are going to be days that I want to stay in bed and talk to no one, but with God and my family behind me, I will be just fine. I refuse to go backwards and as Dory sings, "Just keep swimming!" Everybody calls me Dory because I forget everything, just like the fish Dory in the Disney movie. I laugh it off. I realized that I might be living with Lyme the rest of my life, but I won't let that stop me either. I might never get to eat another carb in my lifetime, but when I get to that pearly white gate in heaven, I'm going to be greeted with a heavenly banquet of only the stuff I couldn't eat on earth. I'm looking forward to that.

I still get down on myself at times. Even now I think I'm not a good mother. I didn't have the patience to sit and play games with my kids. I wouldn't take them to the park unless there was an adult with me to talk to. Maybe it was the way I was raised. I know I'm not well mentally. Everyone in my family has some sort of mental illness. I love my kids to death. But I always thought I didn't deserve them. I couldn't understand why I couldn't connect with them like other mothers did with their children. When they were babies, I was a great mother. I loved to hold them and always gave them kisses, maybe too many kisses. I couldn't get enough of them. But when they got older, it was like a switch went off in me. All of a sudden, I couldn't handle them. Everything became such a chore. They all had some kind of difficulty I had to deal with, but so do many other mothers. There are mothers with worse problems than mine. It killed me inside to even think about how I felt at times. There is something in me that is still broken. But God is never going to be done with me. I still and always will be growing and learning. Jesus has become my teacher. I have a long way to go. He has blessed me with these children, and I'm so grateful. I will continue to pray to become the mother I want to be. That has been one of my greatest prayers: to be a great mother. And at times, I am seeing a change in me.

> You belong to God, children, and you have conquered them, for the one who is in you is greater than the one who is in the world. (1 John 4:4)
>
> For such men are false apostles, deceitful workmen, who masquerade as apostles of Christ. And no wonder, for even Satan masquerade as an angel of light. So it is not strange that his ministers also masquerade as ministers of righteousness. Their end will correspond to their deeds. (2 Corinthians 11:13–15)

It feels like the world is falling apart. There are so many evils out in the world. Look at the TV shows the kids watch and the music they listen too. Everything is about sex. We live in the flesh, not in the Spirit. Do you ever see any celebrities happily married? So much divorce out there, they give up too soon. It takes hard work to be married. It takes sacrifice. There are so many young people out there hooking up, like it's no big deal. I really think some of the girls are doing it because of peer pressure. They are not being told by their parents that it's wrong. The culture says it's fine, do whatever feels good. The culture is also trying to take God out of everything, painting us as the bad guys and freaks. We are called haters and all sorts of stuff that is not true. I could have a different opinion about certain things because of my religion, but that doesn't mean I hate someone who doesn't agree with me. Christians are taught to love everyone. God did give us free will. I won't judge anybody, and I wish I wouldn't get judged for my beliefs.

It clearly states in the Bible how we should be acting. God doesn't want to control us. He has given us free will. He wants us to be happy and live our lives to the fullest. But we can't be happy without God, our creator. We were created to love God; we were created in his image. If you truly get to know Jesus in an intimate way, you would fall in love with him; you would gladly change your life. What a wonderful world this would be if we all follow God. It doesn't even matter what religion you are; all of us are God's children. We need more people who have morals. There are people who don't believe in God and have morals. Search your heart and start praying. I pray everybody finds God. The devil is working hard on our families, trying to pull us all apart. We must be warriors and fight for our families. Our goal is to get our families to heaven. Pray for our children every day. Work on your marriages, don't give up. I feel like I'm getting to know James again for the first time. We are experiencing new things together, keeping it fresh and new.

We started to go to a friend's house for a family rosary. They had many families that went. All the children would say a decade of the rosary. Then we would have some fellowship and the kids would play together. It was a great way to keep my kids involved with other believers. And it also kept me from walking away. Because even though I believe in God and seen all his miracles, there are still some days I wish I could walk away. The family is moving to Florida, so with prayer and asking my husband, we decided to keep it alive and have it at our house. It's important to keep me and my family close to God. And we all need a little help from friends to stay in check. It is important for my kids to see that other families are like us so they don't think we are crazy.

> Indeed, the grace of our Lord has been abundant, along with the faith and love that are in Christ Jesus. (1 Timothy 1:14)
> Do not conform yourself to this age but be transformed by the renewal of your mind, that you may discern what is the will of God, What is good and pleasing and perfect. (Romans 12:2)

We tend to get in God's way a lot. We feel we could do it on our own. We think we know what's best for us. All of us need to get out of God's way for him to work on us or on the situation that we are in. If I find myself not able to deal with any situation, I got to say, "Jesus, I can't do this, please take over, fix what I have broken, and turn it into good." He will find a way to make our mistakes a teachable moment. He is always teaching me. He'll always get me through it. Look how far he has taken me. My whole life is a miracle. One example of getting out of God's way is when we put our daughter Danielle into a Catholic High School. One night she wanted to go to the movies with her friends. James and I were on our way to a restaurant for date night. We were still in the car parked. James didn't want her to see this movie; he didn't think it was appropriate. There were times I would argue with him about what I thought was okay for her to see. But this time I kept my mouth shut and all I did was pray. He wound up calling her friend's father to ask him what he thought about it. Her father told him that we did a good job in raising our children and now it was time to let them go a little and let them out in the waters and see where that brings them. He trusted this man because he was a godly man. Instead of me and James getting into a fight over it, God took care of it for me. He got off the phone and decided to let her go. I turned my head to the car window looked up and said, "Wow, you work fast!" And I thanked God. I said this in my head, not out loud of course. I witnessed this so many times in my marriage. Sometimes I just got to shut my mouth and let God take over, which is very hard for me. I don't like to keep quiet when I think I'm right, which is often.

Chapter Thirty-One

So whoever is in Christ is a new creation: the old things have passed away; behold, new things have come. (2 Corinthians 5:17)

I have had a weird and difficult life with many ups and downs. Sometimes I can't believe I made it through. Just think of what would have happened to me if I didn't have God in my life. My life could have ended up so bad, could have even ended in death. How much can one person handle? Well, I'll tell you, you can handle anything when you put your trust in God.

Everything happens for a reason. I believe everything had to happen the way it did, good and bad, for my life to end up in the place I am now. If even one thing was prevented, my life would have been different. It had to be this way. The suffering I had to go through and still go through need to happen. It is making me the person I am. It's molding me into the person I'm supposed to be. And even though I don't have a good image of myself most of the time as a mother and a wife, I know I'm a good-hearted person. God loves me the way I am but also wants me to be more.

That good heart doesn't always come out with my family. Sometimes I can be harsh with them. I always regret it afterward. And I always say I'm sorry to my kids when I haven't been very nice to them, always asking for their forgiveness, and them always forgiving me. I heard somewhere that it is easier to show love to others than it is to show love to your family. I think that's because your with them all the time, they are the closest people to you. It's easy to get mad and annoyed at them sometimes. They are the people you love the most.

God is full of surprises; he never ceases to amaze me. Two things God surprised me with was homeschooling my kids and writing this book. I hated school, and I also hated to read. He surprised me with other stuff too, like having more children when all I wanted was two. Living in a house, which I never thought in a million years I would own a house. He is making me stronger.

But even now while writing this book, I'm having doubts. Will this book ever get published? Am I good enough to write a book? Am I living in a fantasy? What am I thinking, trying to write this? Is it for me, others, or God? Are these my insecurities or the evil one in my head? I'm being attacked.

I went to a Charismatic Conference not too long ago. I came out of it with the knowledge that God loves the person I am and I should never be afraid of anything. I felt so much power, like the Holy Spirit jumped right into me. I felt free, like I could do anything I put my mind to, as long as it was done for the glory of God. I had to put God in everything I did, little or big. But of course, I would get attacked right after, with fear.

I will never be perfect, and I should know that and be okay with it. I have met some wonderful new families that are trying to live a Christ-centered life, and it has been wonderful spending time with them. We went to a fest that had Christian singers. There was Mass done outside and lots of praise and worship. All these things bring me closer to God, and being at the conference made me realize how much I miss community life. I need people to hold me accountable, to go to conferences with, Abby Fests, and to go on pilgrimages, like we used to. We all need community. We need people we can count on to call us out when we are not praying or putting God first.

Believing in God and trying to live according to his will doesn't mean everything is going to be peachy in your life. We all are going to have trials. We are always going to be tempted to do the wrong thing. And there will be many times we fail. But God is always there; he always will love us and always will be ready to forgive us if we ask him to. We will be weak at times, but he can make us stronger if we ask him to. He allows us to go through trials and pain for a reason. Sometimes it's just to teach us something about ourselves, and other times, it's to make us stronger. We really don't know why, but there is a reason.

It's easy to give up on him when you're in a lot of pain spiritually, physically, or mentally. But keep trusting in him to get you through it. He won't let you down in the end. After all my trials, I have seen what God was trying to tell me. But when you're in the thick of it, you can't see it. You just got to trust that God will be there for you and help you through it.

Chapter Thirty-Two

Put on then, as God's chosen ones, holy and beloved, heartfelt compassion, kindness, humility, gentleness, and patience, bearing with one another and forgiving one another, if one has a grievance against another; as the Lord has forgiven you, so must you also do. And over all these put on love, that is, the bond of perfection. (Colossians 3:12–14)

To sum it all up, God has been very good to me. Through all my ups and downs, he has never left my side. God opened my eyes up to new possibilities. I am enjoying the new me. God has made me see that I shouldn't fear anything. Things that I have never done before, I'm doing now. He has given me the courage to do the small things as well as the big ones, like cheering at my daughter's soccer game (which I would never do before) to writing this book.

I'm enjoying watching football with my husband and becoming a crazy Cowboy's fan. Going golfing with my husband and being so bad at it but having fun. God has given me courage beyond anything I could ever imagine. I'm experiencing new ways to have fun with my husband. I won't let anything stop me, even when I feel sick from my Lyme. I'm going to live the rest of my life to the fullest. I'm checking things off my bucket list. I was a frightened little girl before; now I'm feeling stronger because of God. I didn't always get what I prayed for, or when I did, it didn't come in my time. I'm a very impatient person. I never like waiting for anything. Some things are worth waiting for. God showed me the way, and I took it.

God has healed me in so many ways. God has allowed me to love myself so I could be able to better love others. God showed me all people are sinners and need to be loved no matter what. I don't have to always like everybody or like what they do, but I must love them and show love and compassion to all. I know what I need to do to love my family and treat them right. He has given me the tools.

That doesn't mean I'll never fall. I will fall a lot, but now I know who to go to for help. Writing this book has been a healing for me. It showed me all the times God has been in my life. I'm grateful for God's love, mercy, and forgiveness. I wasn't always good to him. I don't know where I would be without him. I want to go deeper and deeper with him. I want to know everything about him. I want to love him more.

> In all circumstances give thanks, for this is the
> will of God for you Christ Jesus. Do not quench
> the Spirit. (1 Thessalonians 5:18)

I'm grateful to my husband who always stuck by me through all my lows, and I had a lot of them. James is the best man I know. I love him with all my heart, and now I know what love is. It's not just a feeling. It's a willingness to put that person first. Not to give up on a relationship when it gets too tough. To love that person even on the days you don't feel like it. And to pray, pray, pray for your spouse. Pray together. Pray with the whole family. Be grateful for all you have. There are no better riches than God and a family. Things come and go, but your family is forever. And God will never leave you; I'm rich with this knowledge. I have spiritually come from rags to riches.

> For by grace you have been saved through faith,
> and this is not from you; it is the gift of God,
> (Ephesians 2:8)

About the Author

D awn Large grew up in New York City. Then her family moved to Brooklyn. She now lives in New Jersey with all her children still at home.

She has been married to her first true sweetheart for thirty-three years. They met in Brooklyn, New York, when she was thirteen and he was fourteen. She knew the first time she set eyes on him, he was the one.

She has four children: Joseph is thirty-three, Dana is twenty-six, two adopted children, Andrew is fourteen and is from South Korea, and JoyAnna is ten and from China. She has two children in heaven, Gianna and Lucy. She also has two furry children, her dogs Ruby and Max.

This is Dawn's first book. She felt God wanted her to write this book, and she had a willingness to help others.

She and her husband had helped other young couples with the experience of their marriage. They would counsel them on raising children, finances, drug abuse, and struggles with intimacy. This was all done by telling them their stories.

She has had health problems and has turned to natural remedies. Because of that she is now selling natural supplements, trying to teach others how important it is to take care of their bodies and know what they are putting into their bodies.

Her personal interests are listening to music, dancing, praising and worshiping God, socializing with others, watching action-packed movies, the Hallmark channel, and vacationing. She loves to be with family and friends.

CPSIA information can be obtained
at www.ICGtesting.com
Printed in the USA
FFHW022352280619
53279553-58973FF